TimeS~~a~~

A Posit~~iv~~e ~~P~~sychology
Approach to ADHD

Virginia M. Hurley Ed.D.

Table of Contents

Acknowledgements: Gratitude and appreciation go to my family, who richly deserve every good thing.

For their expert editorial and content help, a special portion of appreciation goes to Jeannie and Debbie. Thank you for your prodigious talents and loving-kindness. I can savor the experience now because a cup of tea tastes good.

Introduction: THIS BOOK IS ABOUT how to savor time through Positive Psychology coaching. For those with time management and ADHD issues, this is a strengths-based approach to their struggles with time. Among many areas for improvement, people frequently seek coaching support for prioritizing, timeliness, focus, goal setting and completion, motivation, and improved relationships. Using a Positive Psychology time perspective, narrative, along with exercises in gratitude, and savoring, change clients' focus from "what goes wrong" to what can be "even better if." From the outset, "Time Savor" coaching asks the question, "What are you good at?" This style of coaching evolved through researched based methods from Positive Psychology, particularly in the areas of Appreciative Narrative, Gratitude, and Savoring. This is a unique coaching approach that helps those with ADHD develop reachable goals, de-cluttered agendas, and an overall boost in wellbeing.

TimeSavor Coaching incorporates 3 major ways to focus on Strengths:

Appreciative Narrative: Telling the story of a time of success -your best moment—your ideal results—your best possible self—writing about the worst and the best outcomes

Gratitude: Recalling what goes right—connecting to something greater than yourself—having more positive emotions—dealing with adversity

Savoring: Learning positive reminiscence—mindfulness in the present—optimistic anticipation

TimeSavor Coaching does focus on personal strengths but not to the exclusion of current weaknesses. Seen together, they increase clients' ability to design and keep goals, by:

Using assessments from Positive Psychology

Underscoring the ability to do "even better if…."

Using researched-based strategies in novel ways

Addressing the major issues with clarity, brevity, and simplicity

Developing awareness and accountability

Looking closely at self-management and social awareness

Questioning and Changing

Chapter 1

WHERE DOES IT HURT?

What do most people think they already know about those with Attention Deficit Hyperactivity Disorder (ADHD)? What do they think they already know about people with time management problems similar to those of people with ADHD? It's been said from time to time that for people like this, nothing will ever change with them.

Time management issues, particularly problematic for many individuals with ADHD, occur because people choose to act the way they do. Perhaps some have felt quite strongly that ADHD is not a "real" medical condition, but is caused by poor parenting early on. Really, some will say, people like this are either not very smart or are very lazy. Or, is it just possible that people with time management or ADHD just use this as an excuse for the way they go through life, as others may suspect? In fact, some will add, there's really no upside for people like this. They are in a box of their own making. There is surely room for improvement, but consistent improvement is very elusive.

Every statement above represents a common misunderstanding that stigmatizes and stifles perfectly fine people having perfectly awful struggles. They are all part of the myths behind ADHD in adults.

An article by Dr. Phyllis Anne Teeter Ellison, former president of CHADD (Children and Adults with Attention Deficit/ Hyperactivity Disorder), does an excellent job bringing facts to the assumptions made by the general public. In her article, "AD/HD Myths: Science Over Criticism" (2003) Teeter Ellison first tackles the myth that AD/HD is not a real disorder. There is widely-accepted evidence in the medical community that ADHD behaviors have a strong impact on other aspects of social, emotional, academic, and work functioning, and are frequently related to issues of depression, anxiety, and personality disorders. These occurances are much highter in those with ADHD than in the general population. The concensus among those in the medical profession, then, is that ADHD conditions as such constitute a mental disorder.

There is, however, a stronger body of evidence that has emerged recently. In addition to previous links with mental disorders, we now know much more about brain functioning through technolgy developed to observe the brain at work. Dan Amen, psychiatrist and clinical neuroscientist, has worked for many years using the SPECT scan (Single-Proton Emission Computed Technology) and has written extensively on his findings, notably in <u>Change Your Brains, Change Your Mind</u> (1998). Amen and colleagues found through scan data that there is not just one type of ADHD. The constellation of symptoms that are included in the diagnosis of ADHD are represented in different areas of the brain map. But in all cases, SPECT images show a brain that is working inefficiently, activating more than the usual number of neurological structures for thinking, communicating, and remembering. More will be said about ADHD and the brain in Chapter 8.

Teeter Ellison (2003) also takes issue with the myth that poor parenting <u>causes</u> ADHD. While she does suggest that poor parenting in the form of unrelenting criticism, negativity, and domination do exacerbate defiant and uncooperative behaviors, this is true of most children, not just those with attentional issues. Teeter Ellison holds the theory that research is much more supportive of genetic factors involved in the causation of ADHD, occuring more frequently and being more discernable than parenting differences. Other factors, besides the highly heritable nature of ADHD, include in some but not all cases, exposure to toxins and poor nutrition, as noted in her article.

Hallowell and Ratey, in <u>Answers to Distraction</u>, (1994) take a similar view, that parenting styles do not cause ADHD. They agree that ADHD is not a mythical fad, but a medical diagnosis. They understand, however that it is a real brain difference. Hallowell and Ratey note that we are coming closer to an ability to diagnosis ADHD using technology such as the fMRI and SPECT scans as used by Dan Amen. While brain studies thus far have shown small differences in the structure of the ADHD type brain compared to that of symptom free individuals, these small physiological differences represent significant behavioral differences. These differences have been recognized in the brain's "corpus callosum," the area responsible for the smooth flow of communication between the brain's two hemispheres. This may explain why some people with ADHD also have significantly slower processing of information. But, to be sure, this has no relationship to the relative intelligence of those with ADHD. Nor is slower processing really caused by character flaws, such as laziness.

Can ADHD symptoms be improved? Most definitely they can. Educators and other practitioners have developed a body of practice to include interventions for such behaviors as those relatd to inattention, hyperactivity, impulsivity, and goal development and goal completion. Stephen B. McCarney, for example, has developed a classic intervention manual (1994) that has been used to develop educational and workplace plans for those with ADHD. Carney was an early advocate of creating environments free of distractions, and of adding meaning to activities that matched the motivational styles of students and workers He also promoted the important concept of "chunking" long-term projects into manageable tasks. He early on recognized the importance of having someone take on a coaching role, especially to help those with ADHD explore better ways of doing things. In fact, a plan with structure, meaning, autonomy, and competence, such as that described in Deci and Ryan's Self Determination Theory (2002) provides successful interventions for ADHD clients, along with newer models of interventions from the disciplines of coaching and Positive Psychology.

Where does it hurt? The short answer is: in the mind and heart. What hurts the most? Sufferers say, being misunderstood. The longer answers can be heard below in the stories of just two of many very bright, successful, powerful people. They had their tears in common, and their tears underscored where it hurts. Both called for coaching help after they were diagnosed as adults with ADHD, and the depth of pain it brought amazed them both. Their names have been changed, and some of the stories below are composites.

"Jack" had been a successful self-employed IT consultant for over a dozen years. A desire to start a family and obtain health insurance led him to obtain a project manager job at a very well known international firm in New York City. For the first time, someone else was his boss. His initial attempts at managing others met with sharp criticisms for lateness of product, confusing, incomplete communication, missing information, missing the point of the project's outcome, and failure to capture the specifications of a very important client. Just five months into the job, Jack was a failure in his own eyes, and in the eyes of his bosses and client. Jack sought medical help. He was stunned and speechless at the results. He was diagnosed with ADHD, along with anxiety and depression. He had never even entertained the thought that he could have ADHD, and he began a vigorous campaign to understand what it meant.

A few weeks after the diagnosis, when Jack called to explore coaching, he astonished himself by starting to cry. He described them as "combination tears" of relief, and then of other strong emotions. He finally had a diagnosis that he felt was so much better than what he thought about himself since childhood. He spoke of always being out of step with his peers, of starting trouble in the classroom from Day 1. When he recalled the singular moment that best described the recurring hurt he felt with every defeat, he spoke of getting kicked out of Mrs. Wilson's first grade class. She didn't want him; he "couldn't make it." He was so ashamed to be placed in the *other* first grade. From that moment on, no matter what successes he experienced, he thought of himself as one who "couldn't make it." Ultimately, he was removed from many other classrooms in many other schools, never understanding what worked for him, how to use already developed strengths, how to nurture as yet unrealized capacity. Tears fell again. This time, Jack's "combination tears" were of shame, and frustration, and seething, red-hot anger.

Until that point, he felt that no matter what improvements he tried to make, in behavior, scholarship, or self-regulation, he always missed the mark. To Jack's great shame, his father always interpreted his shortcomings as deliberate acts designed specifically to gain copious amounts of negative attention. Jack absorbed the message from his father that his irreversible defect resided in Jack's character and basic stupidity. And so, Jack cried tears of loss and grief. He was neither bad, nor stupid after all. He was, rather, a man whose brain worked very differently than that of many -but not all- other people.

New client "Nikki" also phoned in tears, just a few days after her ADHD diagnosis. She, like Jack, had a further diagnosis of depression and anxiety. Her tears, like Jack's, came as a flood of relief. At last, simply knowing the name of what made her different brought a sort of peace. There was a real neurological reason, she exclaimed, to identify what was going on inside her head. She was reading everything she could about ADHD. She was very impressed that there were others, too, who shared her way of perceiving the world. She cried again, because she "wasn't an alien being." Her diagnosis gave her unexpected footing on a planet she thought belonged to everyone else but Nikki.

Now, Nikki was a very successful woman, with incredible grades and accomplishments, but all that came at a very high mental, physical, and emotional price. She cried, then, in frustration at the seemingly unnecessary struggles she went through to create her considerable academic and professional gains. "No one ever helped me!" she protested. "Why didn't anyone ever teach me how to manage this?" She was furious. "You mean, people knew about ADHD, and about ways that could have helped me all along? Why didn't anyone ever tell me about this? I never thought I had ADHD. I NEVER EVEN KNEW ABOUT IT."

Around this same time, she met by chance a very favorite elementary school teacher. It took a moment for the teacher to recognize Nikki, but when she did, here were her first words:

"Oh Nikki, you were such a brat! I dreaded teaching the class with you in it! Oh, I loved you dearly, but you were impossible to control!"

Where does ADHD hurt? Jack and Nikki shared the depth of pain created by the unthinking words of others, notably a father and two teachers that became the foundation of a criticizing inner narrative for each of them. The amount of mental energy each of them donated to placating their highly developed inner critics robbed them of capacity for a sense of wellbeing. They were certainly capable of finding enjoyment and meaning in life, yet they each said that wasn't happening for them, as Time itself was such an enemy. Both of them were deeply invested in the "Bad Person" narrative, so much so that it left no room for Jack and Nikki to explore their strengths and enjoy that sigh of relief that comes from a sense of competence and accomplishment. Although both worked hard to succeed, the essence of gratification and gratitude seemed to miss the core of their beings. They were left with feelings of isolation and alienation. They came to coaching ready to make some big changes.

Chapter 2
WHAT ARE THE ISSUES?

"All your life, you've been lazy."

"Have you ever heard of a calendar?"

"What's wrong with your alarm clock?"

"You've never had any will power."

"All you have to do is just sit down and don't move until you get this finished!"

What else have you heard people say about those who consistently disappoint them in the areas of time management, with or without an ADHD diagnosis? Just as Jack and Nikki had reasons for tears, so do those who live with, work with, play with, love, and befriend those who react to time as though it were a surrealistic painting.

A call to my coaching line provided a first-hand example of reasons for tears. It was The Wife. At 10:00 pm one particularly grim winter's night, I answered the phone. The caller was already engaged in a vociferous argument with someone else on her side of the conversation. I thought, " I don't think this is a coaching call. This sounds like a mental health referral." Accusations and ultimatums flew back and forth, but I had yet to be recognized by the caller! After some rather endless moments, the yelling woman realized I had answered the phone and was "live." "Oh," she said. "I thought I'd get a machine at this hour."

The bottom line was that the marriage would break up if "Tom" the Husband didn't get help for his time management problems, preferably that very night. The Wife bemoaned with vigor and volume that this man dawdled so frequently and so pervasively, she couldn't stand him under her feet one more day. She would call him for breakfast each day, and he would say, "Be right there!" yet never actually show up. In fact he missed so many meals, not just breakfast, she was ready with the ultimatum: show up ON TIME ALL THE TIME, or get out for keeps. The Wife said coaching was the last resort. Tom was on medication. He had been to therapy. The outcome was the same: "Be right there!" The Wife was on even more medication, was seeing a therapist even more frequently, and she knew this was Tom's last chance.

I spoke to Tom at last. And what was Tom doing when he was supposed to join The Wife for meals and other engagements? Tom was hyper focused on the computer! And did Tom think there was a problem? Well, he knew The Wife was upset, but he couldn't figure out why. In fact, Tom told me that night that he was very happy with himself and didn't want to change. What was The Wife's problem anyway?

Although this is not an exhaustive list by any means, here are some of the issues that bothered The Wife and others. These are the Top Eight ADHD coaching issues I've encountered:

Procrastination
Time-clutter
Self-Management
Inattention and Forgetfulness
Goal Completion
Prioritizing
Relationships

AD/HD and COACHING

The International Coach Federation (ICF) is a certifying body for coaches. The ICF has developed competency standards for coaches based on objective competency standards for other professionals, such as therapists. The code of ethics adhered to by certified coaches is based on those standards as well. ICF certification includes a requirement for specific training in 11 core competencies, and hours of supervision. Oral and written exams are required in order to qualify for certification. Certification is renewed every three years, and must be applied for with evidence of 40 additional hours of coach training for Continuing Coach Education Units, and an additional ten hours of receiving coaching by a professional- or master's-level coach. The following lists the 11 ICF coaching competencies, which can be found at the ICF website: (International Coach Federation, 2011) http://www.coachfederation.org/icfcredentials/core-competencies/

A. SETTING THE FOUNDATION
1. Meeting ethical guidelines and standards
2. Establishing the coaching agreement

B. CO-CREATING THE RELATIONSHIP
3. Establishing trust and intimacy with the client
4. Coaching presence

C. COMMUNICATING EFFECTIVELY
5. Active listening
6. Powerful questioning
7. Direct communication

D. FACILITATING LEARNING AND RESULTS
8. Creating awareness

9. Designing action plans

10. Planning and goal setting

11. Managing progress and accountability

In an article for <u>Attention!</u> entitled "Just What Is Coaching?" (Young & Giwerc, 2003) Joel L. Young and David Giwerc explore the development of ADHD coaching becoming part of the protocol for treatment of clients with ADHD. The standards set by the ICF, they note, are followed. Added to these standards are further specialized courses in working with specific ADHD issues. In order to address cycles of failure that burden adults with ADHD, Young and Giwerc recommend that, in concert with medication and therapy, coaching provides a specialized service in problem-solving, developing strategies based on the client's own strengths and pressing needs. Coaches hold the client's agenda, as one of the most important principles espoused by ICF. This is a powerful service for those who forget what it is they need to do, become distracted and tangential, or impulsively abandoned projects as part of a habit of dealing with stress and challenge. Young and Giwerc also feel coaches play an important role in educating clients about ADHD, most especially to help them build awareness regarding the ways in which symptoms frustrate them. Focus is another area in which coaches are able to help the client develop strategies that can overcome distractions and hold goals much more effectively. Young and Giwerc feel that coaching is a reliable way to bridge the gap between the biological realities of ADHD and the behavioral changes that are possible through skills development, education, and better ways to make choices.

Those who come to coaching have absorbed the toxic message that they ARE procrastinators, time wasters, and so on. If we begin to understand at least some of what hurts, then, what makes it better? This leads to a new kind of refocus, using what we've learned from Positive Psychology Coaching in the areas of Appreciative Narrative, Gratitude, and Savoring.

Chapter 3
POSITIVE PSYCHOLOGY

"Gabe" made his way to TimeSavor Coaching through grief over the tragic loss of one of his young employees. Gabe was a very physically active, hard-working, no-nonsense, 47 year old man of few words. He felt at his best when he was on the move. Without warning, he was stopped in his tracks by his young worker's sudden death. His grief response surprised his family, his friends, and his co-workers, and they were very worried. It was as though a house of cards collapsed. They convinced Gabe to seek help. Among other psychiatric issues, the diagnosis that jumped out at Gabe was that of ADHD.

Gabe called because his psychiatrist recommended coaching to help him manage his ADHD symptoms. He choked back tears during his first conversation, for the untimely death of a young associate, but also because he had ADHD, and as he put it, "Something is wrong with my brain. I am mentally ill." He described how stigmatized he felt because of ADHD. While his grief was resolving and his depression improving, he felt that the ADHD diagnosis was a life sentence of abnormality.

At this point, Gabe didn't know how to handle himself at work because he had a terrible diagnosis related to his brain. Something was officially wrong with him. What would his employees think? Gabe chose TimeSavor Coaching for its Positive Psychology, strengths-based approach. This kind of coaching wasn't predominantly about what was wrong with Gabe; it was very much about what was right with him.

What constitutes "Positive Psychology"? The International Association of Positive Psychology (IPPA), describes Positive Psychology as "...The scientific study of what enables individuals and communities to thrive" (2009). Robert Biswas-Diener, coach, author, teacher, and Positive Psychology researcher states in his book, <u>An Invitation to Positive Psychology</u> (2008) that Positive Psychology "...is the scientific study of human flourishing, and an applied approach to optimal functioning" (2008, p. 5). The Harvard Medical School's <u>Special Health Report on Positive Psychology</u> (Siegel, 2009) notes that Abraham Maslow first coined the term "positive psychology" in the 1950s as part of his understanding of self-actualization, growth, and pursuit of meaning in life.

Positive Psychology does not replace the diagnostic and treatment model most appropriate for mental illness. Rather, it is also part of what makes up human wellness. Biswas-Diener further notes that Positive Psychology as a research-based other arm of psychology, owes its name and initial impetus to Martin E.P. Seligman. Professor of psychology and director of the Positive Psychology Center at the University of Pennsylvania, Seligman asked, "What goes right with people?" (2008). Christopher Peterson (2006), psychology professor at the University of Michigan and one of the original Positive Psychology researchers notes that, although Positive Psychology has deep roots in the disciplines of psychology, philosophy, and religion, it has existed explicitly as an identifiable perspective since 1998.

This new paradigm was articulated by Seligman at the start of his term as president of the American Psychological Association in 1998 (2002). He thought about the post-World War II legacy of depression, and of the many cases of trauma. The resulting modern emphasis in psychology became a more problem-focused study, adapting a diagnostic stance similar to that of the medical model. Seligman proposed rounding out research and practice in psychology, making both more complete, by including mental health along with mental illness.

In the case of ADHD, Hallowell and Ratey (Answers to Distraction, 1994) strongly agree with including the mental health of clients along with the negative traits. In fact, they have chronicled the movement of approaches to ADHD from a moral evil, to an illness, to current thinking that it is a set of traits within a different kind of mind (Hallowell E. & Ratey, 2006). ADHD has been given a medical model definition, as a neurological syndrome characterized by "distractibility, impulsivity, and restlessness" (1994, p. 3). True to the approach of Positive Psychology, many things go right with people displaying these behaviors, and Hallowell and Ratey endorse this description enthusiastically. Help is available through Positive Psychology science and strategies. Individuals can learn to re-narrate their personal stories, appreciating many things that go right for them, the things to be grateful for, and the things to savor in the past, present, and future. These are areas wherein Positive Psychology can make a great contribution in their flourishing.

Martin Seligman followed through on answering what goes right with people by studying a multitude of sources and traditions that dealt with concepts of virtues, "the good life," and other rewarding, fulfilling aspects of life (2002). In 2004, he and Christopher Peterson compiled this extensive research into their seminal work, Character Strengths and Virtues: A Handbook and Classification (2004). This classification became known as the now-famous Values in Action (VIA) Signature Strengths. According to Peterson and Seligman, this classification lists 24 strengths contained within six virtue categories: wisdom, courage, humanity, justice, temperance, and transcendence (2004).

In his classic, A Primer in Positive Psychology (2006), Chris Peterson described how he and fellow researchers concentrated on five, soon-to-become-classic, Positive Psychology exercises. These five exercises provide the strengths-based foundation of TimeSavor coaching. They helped ADHD coaching clients develop a new self-narrative through gratitude for the good people and things in their lives (Emmons, 2007). More gratitude and less anger equaled a positive view of the world and those in it. Appreciative Narrative (Kelm, 2005) is a strong component of these five seminal exercises, as is recognition and appreciation of personal strengths (Seligman, 2002). This awareness building has the potential to neutralize habits of defeat and self-sabotage often present in ADHD coaching clients (Solden, 1995).

The Positive Psychology exercises will be explained a greater length in a later chapter. For now, five exercises are as follow:

1. One of these classic exercises is The Gratitude Visit, for which participants write and deliver a letter of gratitude, reading it aloud to the recipient.

2.   Secondly, participants record Three Good Things every day for a week.

3.   A third exercise tested and validated by Peterson and his colleagues is called You At Your Best.

4.   The fourth exercise is Identifying Signature Strengths, and is basic to building awareness of positive identity

5.   The fifth and final classic Positive Psychology exercise tested by Peterson and colleagues was Using Signature Strengths in a Novel Way.

"Appreciative Narrative" is also described within the Positive Psychology strengths framework (Orem, 2007). Appreciative Narrative is related to the character strength of "wisdom." Using Appreciative Narrative develops enhanced perspective by increased attention to the positivity found in the self and others. It is also related to the strength of "humanity," in the form of "kindness," taking care of one's self through a new, more positive point of view. Likewise, "Gratitude" can be seen as an aspect of the character strength "transcendence," in that it describes the human desire to connect to meaning greater than oneself and to a larger universe (Peterson & Seligman, Character Strengths and Virtues: A Handbook and Classification, 2004). Finally, Bryant and Veroff in Savoring: A New Model of Positive Experience (2007), studied "savoring," a positive experience, building on Seligman's work on authentic happiness (2002). Savoring is also related to the strength of "transcendence" as appreciation of beauty and excellence, and to the strength of "courage," in an approach to life with "vitality," in the form of enthusiasm and energy (Peterson C., 2004).

What goes right with people troubled by behaviors associated with ADHD is a significant theme in the research and work of Drs. Hallowell and Ratey, respected experts in the field. In their book, <u>Delivered from Distraction</u> (2006), their emphasis is getting the most out of life, a signature theme of Positive Psychology. They further encourage consideration of ADHD as a trait, rather than a disorder, when the troubling symptoms can be managed. The "pathology," they point out "...represents only one part of the total picture" (2006, p. 23). What represents the rest of the picture, not considered in a diagnostic medical model?

Hallowell and Ratey (2006) list a number of characteristics that are positive attributes in the lives of those with ADHD. First among positive attributes are many creative talents, some of which are only realized after an ADHD diagnosis. Thinking outside the typical linear-sequential logic is another attribute, along with a way of looking at life in general in an original way. A quirky sense of humor and an unpredictable approach round out the list of different thinking styles, and are for the most part, endearing rather than annoying to others. Hallowell and Ratey (2006) add that many with ADHD are known for having a highly intuitive style. They are people of resilience and persistence, and are often warm and generous as well.

Positive Psychology, then, does not replace the diagnostic and treatment model of psychology, but adds to the picture of mental health by studying what goes right with people. Positive Psychology supports current views of ADHD among some experts. ADHD is considered by some to be a series of traits, rather than a moral failing, character flaw, or illness. Like Positive Psychology, those who coach ADHD clients, especially in the case of TimeSavor coaching, also ask what traits and skills go right for clients, then build on strengths through exercises in appreciative narrative, gratitude, and savoring, among many others.

Chapter 4
POSITIVE PSYCHOLOGY COACHING

Applied Positive Psychology found a home in the coaching profession. In his book, <u>Flourish: A Visionary New Understanding of Happiness and Well-Being</u>, Seligman (2011), recounted how he took Positive Psychology beyond the university classroom, to coaching professionals with a background in the helping professions. Many coaches were already using Positive Psychology principles without knowing it. They routinely asked, "What goes right with people?" They already helped clients seek positive goals and bring out their best (Biswas-Diener R. Dean, B., 2007). Both Positive Psychology and coaching assume that people are, for the most part, "...healthy, resourceful, and motivated to grow (2007, p. 11)." Martin Seligman worked with Ben Dean (www.mentorcoach.com) to develop a coaching program with specific training in Positive Psychology.

What does Positive Psychology coaching look at in particular? Seligman (2011) notes in his book, <u>Flourish</u> that Positive Psychology provides coaching with the theory and the science it needs to develop as a profession. Coaching provides Positive Psychology with the application of theory and science.

What is Seligman's idea of theory, as presented in <u>Flourish</u> (2011)? He uses the anagram, PERMA. The essence of Positive Psychology is positive emotion, engagement, good relationships, finding meaning in life, and accomplishments (2011, p. 70). This is a particularly solid theory for the use of narrative, gratitude, and savoring coaching clients with ADHD behaviors around time management. All three of these Positive Psychology applications facilitate the shift from negative self-talk and self-sabotaging behaviors.

A well-researched support for PERMA (Seligman, Flourish: A Visionary New Understanding of Happiness and Well-Being, 2011) comes from <u>The Handbook of Self Determination Theory</u> (Deci & Ryan, 2002). Self Determination Theory, (SDT), suggests that subjective wellbeing and productivity in the work place are best served when three elements are present in the lives of individuals. These three elements of Self Determination are autonomy, competence, and relatedness. "Autonomy" relates to PERMA's "engagement" and "finding meaning in life." Likewise, "Competence" relates to PERMA's understanding of "accomplishments." Finally, the power of "Relationships" is a directly reflected in PERMA's "good relationships."

In the case of clients with ADHD, autonomy relates to the sense of control of choices and destiny. This is a tremendously powerful mind shift for clients with ADHD, who interpret failures as being immutable parts of their inner character. Competence is another revelation, moving clients in the direction of recognizing what works well in their lives. Practicing coaching exercises in narrative, gratitude, and savoring open clients to the prospect of being good at something, grateful for the people and things they already have, and elevated by the undiscovered beauty of the ordinary.

Deci and Ryan's work in SDT is an underpinning of Heidi Grant Halvorson's research in the areas of motivation and success. Her book, Succeed: How We Can Reach Our Goals (Grant Halvorson, 2010), provides very usable practices for TimeSavor coaching clients. Halvorson calls it the "if...then" system. Three elements, evidence strongly suggests, are necessary for goal completion in a timely manner. Grant Halvorson's research indicates that the first element is clients' formulation of a single, discrete, very precise goal. Along with goal formulation comes a statement of the time and day of the week when work on the goal will commence and conclude. The element, however, most responsible for successful avoidance of procrastination is the following: clients are asked to tell where they are going to be located when they work on the goal! Participants who engaged in all three aspects were more than twice as likely to actually succeed in managing their time well.

Along the same lines, TimeSavor coaching routinely asks, "What goes right with people—with ADHD?" How can they begin to talk about the good in themselves? How can they develop gratitude for what went right, what goes right, what can go right? How can they change their brains by learning the power of mindful savoring: positive reminiscences, attention to the present moment, and optimistic anticipation (Bryant & Veroff, Savoring: A New Model of Positive Experience, 2007).

What about the science of Positive Psychology and coaching? Biswas-Diener, in Practicing Positive Psychology Coaching: Assessments, Activities, and Strategies for Success, (2010), notes the importance of being able to use the science of Positive Psychology in the coaching profession, presenting 11 examples of assessments used by coaches. These assessments, he notes, have many characteristics in common. They include empirical validation, wide use, focus on positive human functioning, coaching appropriateness, and are free of charge, easy to administer, and easy to evaluate (2010, p. 101). Biswas-Diener gives full details of the following assessments available to Positive Psychology coaches and others, for use with their clients.

Various authors developed these assessments, all listed in Practicing Positive Psychology Coaching (2010, pp. 104-124). For those assessments with copyrights, information is listed here.

1. Domain Satisfaction Scale—assesses satisfaction in life area

2. SPANE (Scale of Positive and Negative Experience) an overall affect score © January 2009 by Ed Diener and Robert Biswas-Diener

3. Subjective Happiness Scale—assess general levels of happiness © by Sonja Lyubomirsky

4. Meaning in Life Questionnaire (MLQ)—assess what makes life significant

5. Work-Life Questionnaire—identification with similar people's work styles (Wrzesniewski, Rozin, & Schwartz, 1997) .

6. Purposeful Work Scale—measures a person's sense of engagement in the workplace. © 2009 Robert Biswas-Diener and Alex Linley

7. Trait Curiosity and Exploration Inventory-II—measures preferences for seeking novel experiences and for ability to face uncertainty. © 2009 Kashdan, et. al.

8. Savoring Beliefs Inventory (Bryant, Savoring Beliefs Inventory (SBI): A scale for measuring beliefs about savoring, 2009)—measures positivity through savoring past, present, and future moments

9. Work-Style Scale (Biswas-Diener, Work Style Scale, 2009) -distinguishes four distinct types of motivation related to work

10. Authenticity Scale (Wood, Linley, Maltby, Baliousis, & Joseph, 2008)—measures three aspects of authenticity, of being "genuine and true (Biswas-Diener, 2010, p. 121)."

11. Strengths Use Scale (Govindji & Linley, 2007)—assess people's use of strengths in general.

Scientists and researchers in the field look for evidence that a particular intervention or strategy works. As Seligman explains the science of Positive Psychology, "It uses tried-and-true methods of measurement, of experiments, of longitudinal research, and of random assignment, placebo-controlled outcome studies (Seligman, Flourish: A Visionary New Understanding of Happiness and Well-Being, 2011, p. 71)."

Putting the science of Positive Psychology to work was the inspiration for Biswas-Diener and Dean's work, Positive Psychology Coaching (2007). This work was foundational to the focus on strengths building for those with ADHD. Within its chapters, Biswas-Diener and Dean apply the research behind happiness interventions, strengths coaching, goals and relationships.

Coaching interventions for building narratives about one's future and one's best possible self are included in this work (Biswas-Diener & Dean, Positive Psychology Coaching: Putting the Science of Happiness to Work for Your Clients, 2007). Next, strengths coaching utilizes the V.I.A. Signature Strengths assessment (2007, pp. 120-124) as a prime conversation starter. Included also is coaching toward gratitude, a happiness and relationship builder, using validated exercises and strategies. Finally,

Biswas-Diener and Dean amplify the importance of time orientation through strategies and exercises related to savoring.

How does narrative help coaching clients, especially those with ADHD? In <u>Positive Psychology Coaching</u>, (Biswas-Diener & Dean, 2007) background for the use of narrative includes coaching techniques using lists, journals, planners, and inspirational phrases. Taking it a step farther includes more expressive narratives that shift focus from what has always gone wrong in life, especially in regard to ADHD clients, to telling stories of times in the past when things went well. In addition to uncovering under-acknowledged strengths and triumphs, coaching narratives use validated strategies to build future successes.

Biswas-Diener and Dean in <u>Positive Psychology Coaching</u> (2007) advance the idea that the power of gratitude builds capacity for a more positive awareness of clients' inner and outer worlds. Bob Emmons, professor at the University of California, Davis, did the groundbreaking work on gratitude. Emmons' book, <u>Thanks! How the New Science of Gratitude Can Make You Happier</u> (2007) determined an increase in basic levels of happiness, as well as improvement in overall health, among those who practiced gratitude-enhancing exercises over time. Gratitude also provides a boost in connection to others, bringing along with it an attitude of thanks for persons, places, and things, a related power to forgive life's disappointments, and even put aside anger and envy (pp. 107-110). This shift in the inner environment of ADHD coaching clients is pivotal for changing even the brain chemistry related to fear and negativity (Rock & Page, 2009).

Finally, ADHD coaching benefits from validated exercises in savoring. Biswas-Diener and Dean, in <u>Positive Psychology Coaching</u> (2007) explain savoring as a time orientation factor, taking time to reapportion unproductive busyness and time chaos. Bryant and Veroff (Savoring: A New Model of Positive Experience, 2007) developed a definition of savoring as being positive reminiscence, appreciating the present, and optimistic anticipation. Positive Psychology Coaching advances as well the concept of using novel approaches to savoring exercises to "wake clients up, to trying a more intense view of life and giving space to curiosity" (Biswas-Diener & Dean, 2007, p. 155). For ADHD coaching clients, seeking novelty and having hyperfocused curiosity often shows up as problematic, as noted in the ADHD-specific text, Delivered from Distraction (Hallowell & Ratey, 2006). However, Biswas-Diener and Dean (2007) present distractibility as having potential for clients to use natural inclinations and learning differences for their benefit, elevating novelty and curiosity to strengths that build well-being and effective time orientation.

Both Positive Psychology and the coaching profession ask the same basic question: "What goes right with people?" Coaching has welcomed the theory and science of Positive Psychology. Positive Psychology theory and science, in turn, has benefited from the coaching profession as an appropriate and prepared approach to its application. Ultimately, ADHD coaching clients welcome the theory, science, and application of Positive Psychology, in a strengths-based approach to what goes right with their learning and thinking differences.

Barbara Fredrickson, distinguished professor at the University of North Carolina, Chapel Hill, has researched and written about unveiling hidden strengths as a means of moving out of negativity toward positive emotions and flourishing. In her book, Positivity (2009), she discusses research into the "Positivity Ratio" (p. 120), another foundational premise for TimeSavor coaching methods. Fredrickson describes a 3:1 positive-to-negative statements and self-talk as the tipping point between languishing and flourishing. This mathematical ratio was developed through the research of Marcial Losado, who received his doctorate in psychology from the University of Michigan. Losado, an expert at mathematical modeling of group behavior took Fredrickson's theory of the tipping point between languishing and flourishing and developed the 3:1 ratio, now referred to as "The Losado Ratio (pp. 122-130).

How does this awareness of a positive to negative ratio help TimeSavor coaching clients? It becomes a challenge of self-awareness, a goal, and a transformative move toward better relationships. This ratio is not only a key to healing the wounds of criticism and alienation through patterns of self-talk. It is also a significant aid to the underdeveloped communication skills in many of those with ADHD. Building awareness of how negativity "sounds" is a coaching challenge. Helping clients to pivot from negative statements to positive comments goes even deeper. While those with ADHD can be warm and generous, they can also be impulsive with their speech, at times coming across as impatient and hypercritical. This is the point made by Hallowell & Ratey, in <u>Delivered from Distraction: Getting the Most out of Life with Attention Deficit Disorder</u>, (2006). Fredrickson's work on the flourishing tipping point, and Losado's contribution of the 3:1 tipping point ratio, can be exceedingly helpful when used in coaching situations. Toward developing a baseline, valuable for coaching clients, Frederickson has provided a Positivity Self Test in the Appendix of <u>Positivity</u> (2009, pp. 233-234).

Especially in the case of clients with ADHD issues, coaching uses many Positive Psychology Principles. "What goes right with people?" the key question in Positive Psychology research and applied practice, is likewise the core of coaching. Coaching programs with specific training in positive psychology move this idea forward in general. Seligman describes the "essence of Positive Psychology" in his PERMA model of positive emotion, engagement, good relationships, and accomplishments (Seligman, Flourish: 2011, p. 70). TimeSavor coaching moves PERMA forward in the lives of those struggling with ADHD, through coaching strategies in appreciative narrative, gratitude and savoring.

These three aspects of Positive Psychology are readily adapted to standards of professional coaching. Laura Whitworth, Henry Kimsey-House, and Phil Sandahl wrote the book, Co-Active Coaching (1998), a key text used in training Ben Dean's MentorCoach professionals (Biswas-Diener & Dean, 2007). As Martin Seligman noted, in Flourish: A Visionary New Understanding of Happiness and Well-Being, (2011), MentorCoach training emphasizes Positive Psychology.

What is foundational to Co-active Coaching (Whitworth, Kimsey-House, & Sandhal, 1998, pp. 3-5)? In this model, the four "cornerstones" comprising this foundation are:

1. The client is naturally creative, resourceful and whole. Another way of saying this is the now-familiar sentence, "What goes right with people?"

2. Co-active coaching addresses the client's whole life. It focuses on three principals: fulfillment, balance, and process.

3. The agenda comes from the client. The coach makes sure to keep the client's agenda present, helping them focus on the changes they want to make. In Co-active Coaching, clients are helped to narrate their dreams, desires, and hopes, to create their best future and meet their goals.

4. The coaching relationship is a designed alliance. Co-active coaching is based on how the client best works and learns. This alliance, respecting the particular learning differences of

those with ADHD, requires insight and flexibility on the part of the coach, and responsibility and accountability on the part of the client. The client enjoys the power of creating the agenda. The coach supports that agenda through truthfulness and powerful questions.

The change process is an essential dynamic in developing coaching clients' life balance and goal fulfillment. A change theory text widely-used in coach training is <u>Changing for Good</u>, by Prochaska, Norcross, and DiClemente. Studies of over 1000 people led the authors to determine six clear stages of change, that occur, not necessarily in a straight line, but more likely spiral from one stage to another, backward and forward, depending on the client's level of readiness. The six stages of change are (2002, pp. 39-46) :

1. **Pre-contemplation**. The client is thinking about thinking about making some life changes. The story of The Wife and Tom presented earlier, is a good example of The Wife being ready for Tom to change, but Tom just becoming open to the idea. Often, this phase is marked by the client being demoralized and beaten down. The negative inner narrative is most present at this point.

2. **Contemplation**. The client becomes more and more dissatisfied with certain aspects of their lives. They begin to make some vague plans about changing, but are not definite about making commitments. For example, Nathan, previously mentioned, at first thought about changing careers, but it took some time before he was ready to pick a path to follow and find the means to succeed in a re-training process.

3. **Preparation.** In this phase, clients are considering taking action, most likely within the next month. Gabe is a good example of this. It took some time for him to accept his ADHD diagnosis. After he and those close to him accepted that help was needed, Gabe began the search for an ADHD coach.

4. **Action.** This stage is a time of commitment, although "action" is not the equivalent of change itself. A client can decide to take steps to change a behavior, but feelings, attitudes, and awareness constitute change as well.

5. **Maintenance.** This is the stage wherein clients struggle against relapse into the old habits. It is a time for coaches to mark progress with the client, to help amplify the pain of loss of hard won goals, and the sense of challenge that energizes that commitment to changes made. This is a time for coaches of ADHD clients, in particular, to offer skills of motivation It is the phase in which clients may need help to develop alternative plans for follow through, should they grow weary of the tools they have been using for a while. Seeking novelty, as has been noted, is a characteristic of the ADHD brain. It is quite helpful for clients to develop a "Plan B" and even a "Plan C" for variety's sake.

6. **Termination.** This is the goal of automaticity regarding change. Clients have gone through the phases sufficiently to become habituated to the change they desired. For clients with ADHD, like Jack, who placed himself in a new job situation that was highly challenging, entering the termination stage, may at

length, occur. However, Jack, and others like him, return to the maintenance stage from time to time, to the degree that pursuits are less compatible with ADHD-typical behaviors.

The foundation of Positive Psychology coaching comes first from Flourish, and Martin Seligman's idea of "PERMA," that is, positive emotion, engagement, good relationships, meaning and accomplishments (2011). Comfortably supporting PERMA are elements of change theory and Co-active Coaching, as explained in Changing for Good (Prochaska, Norcross, & DiClemente, 2002) and Co-active Coaching (Whitworth, Kimsey-House, & Sandhal, 1998), In addition, assessments, activities, and strategies for bringing out what works well, specific to both Positive Psychology and the practice of coaching add to an understanding of Positive Psychology coaching (Biswas-Diener, 2010).

The TimeSavor coaching model uses this same background in Positive Psychology coaching, merging theories of stength finding with an understanding of special coaching needs of those with ADHD-type behaviors (Hallowell & Ratey, Answers to Distraction, 1994). The focus, then, of the TimeSavor coaching model is to emphasize work in three areas of Positive Psychology, that is, Appreciative Narrative, Gratitude, and Savoring, to build capacity for lasting time management change.

Chapter 5
APPRECIATIVE NARRATIVE

Sing a new song

According to David Cooperrider, in <u>Appreciative Inquiry: A Positive Revolution in Change </u>(2005), it's the question that starts the change. In the case of those with ADHD-like behaviors, a good question to start the change in narrative would be this one: "What's right with people with ADHD thinking?" ADHD thinking is not always a deficit, but can demonstrate strengths as well.

Appreciative Narrative represents a significant focus in Orem's book, <u>Appreciative</u> <u>Coaching</u> (2007), mentioned earlier. Much to the benefit of ADHD-type thinkers, spending the time to practice Appreciative Narrative is related to building the inner strength of wisdom. Exercising and building wisdom helps create strength to balance out impulsivity, frequently associated with ADHD deficit behaviors. Various narrative exercises have been widely applied in coaching sessions. Through insight gained into positive aspects of lives, these coaching clients improve connections with others and build a more supportive and grateful inner-self. While many ADHD-type thinkers show frequent bursts of empathy and kindness, new narratives open possibilities into more consistent and fully developed kindness and care of others.

An interesting benefit of Appreciative Narrative is a new capacity for taking care of one's self through an increase in positivity.

When Hallowell and Ratey (1994) list the desirable traits of having an ADHD-type mind, they were providing a novel point of view to sufferers and families alike. They encouraged a belief in the possibility that attributes could be cultivated. Cultivated attributes could trump deficits more and more consistently over time. Creativity, novel thinking, courage, kindness, seeing the bigger picture, noticing salient details, athleticism, and enthusiasm are among the traits to be celebrated and narrated as well.

Strategies for Narrative

Various exercises in narrative begin with three underlying pivotal questions: What are you good at? What do you need more of? What are your next steps?

This is the essential thinking behind David Coopperrider's phases of Appreciative Inquiry (2005), known as the 4 Ds: discovery, dream, design, and destiny. Further, Orem and her colleagues, writing in Appreciative Coaching (2007), indicate that these phases move at times sequentially, but for coaching clients, they may also move forward and backward, with repeats and reevaluations. The discovery phase is the now familiar, "What goes right with what you do?" The dream stage processes the question, "What do you need more of right now, if you could have all the things you need?" The discovery and dream stages lead to learning about an optimum design for the near and distant future. Finally, the destiny phase leads clients to articulate next steps. What they are going to comit to? What will they take responsibility for?

Such narratives were researched by Laura A. King, of the University of Missouri-Columbia, and by Sonja Lyubomirsky, of the University of California, Riverside. Future oriented narratives encourage clients to imagine their lives in the future, a future in which everything has gone well (King, 2001) (Lyubomirsky, 2007). This is not necessarily an easy venture for ADHD clients, who have difficulty separating their behaviors from their own character and nature. Yet, in trying to describe this future life, clients become open to learning more about what obstacles to overcome and what strengths to use.

Nikki's experience with narrative was very powerful. When Nikki took on the challenge of imagining a future in which everything worked out in the best possible way, she saw herself doing field research, consolidating the expertise she had developed over her lifetime. She saw herself traveling and studying, publishing and presenting, developing a unique brand of health service delivery over time. When she first articulated this dream, she came to a point of self-forgiveness. She was not meant for the conference room, the office cubby, a four-walls type of environment. Yet this was where she found herself for the previous decade. Her best future, by contrast, had her on the move, indulging her great curiosity and love of learning, two of her top signature strengths, along with love and kindness.

Another version of this exercise describes, not so much an ideal future, but an ideal self. Clients are instructed to write about their "best possible self" (2007, pp. 99- 100). Clients again stretch their imagination to learn about those characteristics they value and admire and hope to augment within themselves, toward the ideal. The power of appreciative narrative described here, along with other iterations of focused writing, provide a central coaching principal for ADHD coaching within the Time-Savor model.

Jack and Nathan each had a very difficult time with this exercise. The simple fact of presenting them with this challenge opened up their abilities to express their distance from the notion of being an "ideal self." What came clear over a number of coaching sessions was their sense of disappointment with the role models in their lives. Parents, teachers, friends, older siblings, all of them and more were reduced to painful memories of criticism and belittling. Neither Jack nor Nathan could find a mental image of an ideal self within their immediate circle of relatives and friends.

In that case, the men looked outside that intimate circle to other purveyors of virtue. Jack, for example, found the characteristics of the head of a European company something he could admire. He thought that his ideal self would be decisive, reliable, and productive. The ideal Jack would embody the leadership qualities of the company head, a person he admired from afar. Jack's best possible self, he wrote, would be a much better communicator, listening with greater skill, and speaking in concise details rather than rambling generalities. In creating this self-image, Jack began to re-work his agenda, seeking tools to develop the leadership and communication style he wanted for himself. Jack took skills assessments, read books on leadership, and began to practice tips on effective communication as a result of his narrative attempt.

On the other hand, Nathan's approach to his best possible self started with a litany of his worst characteristics, his worst possible self. Not having access to an idealized model, Nathan began to pivot his negative descriptors, turning them into positive statements about what he longed to become. His best possible self was, then, a fluent reader and adept test taker. Nathan translated this awareness into getting a tutor and developing the skills he desired in reading and testing.

Next, he wrote about his best possible self as being a better friend. Nathan learned some basic communication skills. He found ways to control anxiety when in conflict situations. He became aware of his flight response, and learned simple ways to stay the course with friends. Although seemingly impossible to create, Nathan eventually wrote about his best possible self, thus clarifying his own goals for personal change. Both Jack and Nathan put into action the results of their deepened self-awareness.

Another approach to narrative, a novel one, comes from coach and author Michael Bungay Stanier in his book, Do More Great Work (2010). Bungay Stanier harkens back to the classic story telling style. Its structure is simply: "Once upon a time.... And THEN....Finally...."

This version is a story told twice, having two different elements of rising action and conclusion. TimeSavor Coaching uses this version, since, like Bungay Stanier, it believes in having respect for clients' needs to tell of their fears and reveal their obstacles. Then, clients are encouraged to try on an amazingly optimistic version.

The narrative exercise starts by asking clients to tell the story of a particular goal on their agendas, in which they are the protagonists of "Once upon a time, I..." story. In the first version, everything takes a turn for the worse when the story gets to the "And THEN" section. "Finally," produces the most feared and disasterous outcome the client can imagine.

The narration then becomes one of optimism, allowing the client to recover from the expression of negativity, doubt, and fear, to a more energized imagined outcome. In the second scenario, the "And THEN" part of the tale tells of incredible good results. This is how the story would go if everything possible went right. "Finally" produces the most dearly held and desired outcome, a coaching version of "happily ever after."

Gabe tried this exercise, and surpised himself by the power of narration. In the first version, Gabe told the story of having ADHD in the workplace environment. In this traumatic tale, Gabe was helpless to change his habits of impulsivity, distractibility, blameshifting, and miscommunication. When he got to the "And THEN," he wrote of his behaviors becoming intolerable to his customers and employees. So many mistakes were made, that, "Finally," Gabe lost his livelihood, his relationships, and most of all, his self respect.

In his appreciative version, Gabe took his ADHD into the workplace, but this time it was in the background. What he did was tell the story of his business strengths, even as he was just becoming aware of them. He focused on his contributions and the value he brought to the workplace. "And THEN" he talked about using organizing tools and communication tips, along with taking responsibilty instead of blameshifting. "Finally," his customers and employees grew in satisfaction and loyalty, as did Gabe.

The five classic Positive Psychology exercises below appear in Peterson's book, A Primer in Positive Psychology (2006). They are foundational to the research-based work in narrative, as used by TimeSavor Coaching.

1. The Gratitude Visit: While this precise format is the one tested and validated, other iterations have included writing The Gratitude "Letter" (not "Visit") and sending, rather than delivering, it. When delivering or sending the letter is not possible for any number of reasons, The Gratitude Letter is written

nonetheless, as yet another modification to the original design (Lyubomirsky, 2007).

2. <u>Three Good Things</u>: Study participants were asked to explain why each of the three things went well. This can actually prove challenging to ADHD clients early on. They have to make a conscious shift to go beyond the many things they believe did not go well, in order to focus on just three that did go well. Thinking about why things went well proves to be an insight-builder. ADHD clients, such as those who participate in Time-Savor coaching, begin to build an unconscious inventory of how things go well. In fact, Stanford professor Carol Dweck writes about the advantages of placing information such as this in our unconscious mind in her book, <u>Mindset</u> (2006). Over time, she writes, cues stored in the unconscious take some pressure off the thinking processes. Making things easier for the brain is a very good thing for those with ADHD. Collections of stories about what went right and why are remembered on an automatic level, becoming part of a new repertoire of strength-related behaviors.

3. <u>You at Your Best</u>: The task was to write a story about something that brings out the best in you. The extension to this exercise includes reviewing the story every day for a week. You At Your Best, whose origin can be found in Orem's <u>Appreciative Coaching</u> (2007), has many different titles, but it is a particularly important part of the discovery process for ADHD coaching clients. It is often a challenge for them to find "full voice" in identifying an "at your best" moment. Practice with this process helps.

4. <u>Identifying Signature Strengths</u> (Peterson, 2006): This provides a significant underpinning for the Positive Psychology perspective of the TimeSavor coaching model. Peterson's research participants were asked to take an on-line measure of character

strengths and note their five highest scores. The extension of this exercise was to use these strengths more often in the following week.

5. Using Signature Strengths in a Novel Way: In this exercise, participants made note again of their highest scores on the Signature Strengths Questionnaire (Seligman, 2002). This time, they tried to use their top strengths in a novel way. Novelty is very appealing to the ADHD brain, and variations of this exercise support the paradigm shift from negative and destructive behaviors to those that are more accommodating to wellbeing. Using strengths in a new way adds details to appreciative narrative, to gratitude, and savoring.

Narrative, as used with TimeSavor coaching clients, is an exercise in answering the question, "Why didn't evolution select out the ADHD brain?" Nikki, Jack, and Nathan found themselves able to write about a best possible future and their best possible selves. This was a truly amazing experience for each of them. Their dominant narrative had, up until then, been one of defeat and unhappiness.

Some TimeSavor Coaching Narrative Exercises

"Once Upon a Time..."—tells the imagined story of clients' efforts to reach a dearly held goal. However, the story is told once with both a bad ending and again with a good ending. ADHD clients in particular benefit from an opportunity to connect to consequences and outcomes in this self-generated and emotional way. With coaching help, they increase awareness of obstacles and stumbling blocks unique to their approach to goals. In an energizing and inspiring way, they also recognize, within the "Good Ending" context, opportunities for self-regulation, problem solving, and using their signature strengths in novel ways.

"A Thumbs-Up Moment"—is a positive reminiscence narrative about a time when clients felt successful. Clients are coached to use as many of the five senses as they can to describe this moment, adding enhancement to the memory of success. In coaching sessions, clients are encouraged to explore what they learned about themselves that they could apply to future situations. For clients who have highly developed critical inner narratives, this can be a difficult, yet pivotal, exercise.

"How I Got Ready for My Close-Up"—Clients gets a close look at their own star qualities and allow others to see those qualities as well. This exercise explores signature strengths through the V.I.A. signature strength questionnaire (Seligman, 2002). Clients keep a journal for a week, looking for times during which they recognized the use of one of their strengths.

As an extension, TimeSavor Coaching clients are encouraged to recognize and name strengths they experienced during a subsequent week, especially if the strengths are quite unique to them. For example, Nikki says she has the strength of "radar." She can sense people's moods and needs preemptively and accurately. Nathan discovered he has the strength of "mind space." He can create mental rooms in which to store facts and details. When he "walks" into these rooms, he can "physically find" the information he needs to retrieve! This is a very helpful strength for an ADHD coaching client with debilitating memory problems!

"I Am This, Not That" – This narrative exercise comes from Michael Bungay Stanier's Doing More Great Work (2010). In this exercise, clients create two columns, one with the heading, "I Am This," and the other labeled "I Am Not That." The task is to fill in both columns side by side, with the strength and the deficit in clear visible form. Clients get to choose the way they wish to be authentic through this learning opportunity. They also learn what they would like to demonstrate less of, especially in relationships.

This was a very effective exercise for Gabe, who didn't think he had very much to offer anyone. Although he started out slowly, he picked up enthusiasm for the "I Am This" list. He subsequently designed workplace situations that increased the ratio of "I Am This" to "I Am Not That." His goal, The Losado 3:1 positive to negative ratio!

"Who Do You Say That I Am?"—An extension of this practice for Gabe was to listen to the language Gabe used in his self-talk. His challenge was to listen to the language he used unconsciously to describe himself. He noticed early on that the Losado ratio was not in use. Actually, it was flipped upside down. Gabe was three times more likely to self-describe with words like "stupid," "I'm an ADHD," "forgetful," "slow," "not a good communicator." The pay-off of this challenge was for Gabe to take the language-use awareness one step deeper. What would it be like, then, if Gabe could "pivot" a self-statement like, "I was so stupid again," into something like, "It probably could have been even better if I trusted my judgment more. I can get better at this." Rather than condemn himself, as was his automatic, "default," response, Gabe became more and more willing to learn how to reframe his language.

"Who Do You Say That Gabe Is?" He asked this of himself. Gabe stepped back and said, "Gabe has always been a hard working, honest man. He's not a complainer. He's always ready to lend a helping hand. He's really very good at what he does. He's a loving man. He loves his family and he loves his dog. That's who I say that Gabe is."

"Say Yes To This=Say No To That."—Another exercise from <u>Doing More Great Work</u> (Bungay Stanier, 2010) is a simple equation that helps TimeSavor Coaching clients because it makes so much sense. "Say Yes To This=Say No To That," is the equation. This is a genuine revelation to many with ADHD behaviors, who impulsively say "yes" to too many things to handle. Saying "no" is often not within reach of the decision making part of the brain. Developing awareness of this principle becomes part of an improved decision making process. As the client becomes aware of a decision threshold, that is most typically the "yes" response, the image of this "equation" stirs the subconscious to include awareness of the "no" alternative. In this way, the impulse to say "yes" stirs an unconscious self-regulatory filter that had previously existed in a very weak form, if at all. In time, the word "yes" itself, even in its potential, internal formulation, triggers the STOP response. STOP is followed by the question: What do I lose and what do I gain if I say "no" to this request, or this opportunity? Which answer, "yes" or "no," gets me closest to my deeply held values and preferences? And which answer best matches my availability to take on something else?

Harvard professor Tal Ben-Shahar has expanded this notion in his book, <u>Happier</u> (2007) a work based on his very popular course in Positive Psychology. Ben-Shahar notes that all of us are pulled in many directions, but we do have at least some control over conflicting goals. We don't have to be separated from our happiness and wellbeing by fears, habits, and judgmental criticisms, both internal and external. The capacity to approach a happier state of being, even in those troublesome areas related to time, leaves ADHD clients incredulous at first. Ben-Shahar continues his point, noting that time is a "finite and limited resource" (2007, p. 48), and all of us, most especially those on poor terms with time, need to understand this deeply. Prioritizing comes into play here, but Ben-Shahar is convinced that people can learn to recognize the difference between what is really important and what is less desirable, that is, lower down on their "to do" lists. Here's where self-regulation comes in. This is not easy, and there are many missteps. However, the guiding principal is: "...say 'no' to certain opportunities so that we can say 'yes' to ones that are more valuable to us " (p. 49).

To develop prioritizing skills, Ben-Shahar (2007) suggests avoiding the stressors created by too many changes in routines. This is particularly significant regarding the characteristics of the ADHD brain, which can become derailed from purpose through distractibility related to change. The opposite is also true: changing negative inner narratives and replacing self-defeating habits presents real challenges and truly does not happen overnight. It's helpful, then, to develop habits for those activities people WANT to engage in, like keeping living areas clutter-free, keeping appointments, and finishing projects. It's also helpful to develop time zones in which some negative, time-stealing habits are completely excluded. For example, Ben-Shahar suggests creating things like internet-free time zones for certain times during the day. This habit can also be developed for phone-free time zones, and meeting-free time zones, and TV-free time zones, among many other possibilities. Clients can uncover their own time thieves and create Say Yes to This=Say No To That models that work for them.

The "Yes/No" exercise proved a lifesaver to "Lucy," a Time-Savor Coaching client. Lucy is a successful business owner and single mother of a young family. When she first learned of this "equation," Lucy reported immediate relief from creating her chaotic agendas. She always had idealistic and generous rationales to fall back on whenever she overextended. However, the practice of recognizing that there is a consequence to all her "yes-s" got her to consider important things she <u>lost</u> every time she made an impulsive commitment.

Lucy has a very curious and agile mind. She is talented in many areas of the visual and performing arts, is an athlete, an entrepreneur, and a committed, involved mother of elementary-school aged children. To any observer, it's obvious why her agenda is always full. Knowing that Lucy has a recent diagnosis of ADHD might make it easier to imagine why chaos ruled, no matter how many lists she made, (and lost!), no matter how many agenda programs she downloaded, no matter how many resolutions she made to finish what she started. She sighed, "My plate is too full. Looking at it turns my stomach!" She decided that she would be better off if she could create for herself a small "tapas" plate to replace the Thanksgiving dinner platter she was hauling around with her all day every day! Remembering that "time is a finite and limited resource (Ben-Shahar, 2007), Lucy created this tapas-plate metaphor for her daily planner, and expressed her projects and activities as bite-sized, digestible chunks.

Lucy likes to dream about remodeling plans, visiting multiple web sites to discover information. She uses her artistic skills to sketch out her own ideas. What's wrong with this? As often as Lucy said, "yes" to dreams and fantasies, she was much too frequently saying "no" to important things she wanted as well. Bills went unpaid, corporate clients carried large balances because Lucy neglected to create invoices, and very important communications went unfinished. The remodeling was never initiated, despite Lucy's hours of contemplation. Her unhappiness and self-loathing grew as she lost much more than paper to-do lists and agenda books. Sadly, she lost clients, revenue, and relationships.

Lucy decided to create a two-column chart to work with during coaching sessions. She decided to use this plan to filter out tasks she could delegate. In a triage approach, she would limit her "yes" response to those things that she alone must do. Unsurprisingly, she went on to teach this to her children, creating a communication tool and, and in the process, reducing conflict. While Lucy's "plate" still needs watching, she knows she thrives when she keeps it tapas-sized with little bites.

"Touch It Once"—Lucy very much needed to keep clutter and disorganization away from her brain. To keep things like mail, laundry, and children's toys from piling up and distracting her, Lucy added the "Touch It Once" exercise to her efforts to keep her plate filled with little bites. " Touch It Once" meant that if Lucy put her hand on something, it was to bring it to its final destination then and there. From attempting to do this challenge, Lucy actually <u>created</u> appropriate destinations for her mail, her bills, her laundry, and very significantly, her children's toys. So, if she touched a bill, she was prepared to pay that bill. If she touched junk mail, she was mentally prepared to put it right in the recyclables container she kept exactly where she processed all her incoming mail. In that same area, she kept her <u>labeled</u> file folders and her checkbook, to deal with bills right on the spot. The laundry no longer migrated from dryer to bed, but from dryer to basket to appropriate drawer, as if it were all one process. From practice with narratives, Lucy had a nascent new strength of sequencing, and of applying the notion of "beginning, middle, and end" to her "Touch It Once" challenge. Again, Lucy added value to this exercise by passing it along to her children. She calls it "TIO," for "Touch It Once," and reminds the boys with these initials.

What else can Appreciative Narrative do for coaching clients with ADHD? Narrative, as research suggests, actually does help with time management in other ways as well. Telling important life stories, for example, gives clients practice with beginning-middle-end thinking. This is contrary to tangential, random-thought monologues that often accompany disorganized thinking patterns. This disorganization spills over readily to time-related issues like starting something on time, showing up on time, and finishing up on time. In a related time-sensitive area, narrative boosts clients' ability to tell a story with priorities. What's important? What's extraneous? What do other people need to know about this topic? Practice using this "importance filter" in narratives is very helpful for clearing mental chaos. Even more important, though, is thinking about other people, the audience. This can be a building block for improved empathy. Clients grow in awareness of what is important to others, especially in areas of reliability and timely pursuits.

Coaching with Appreciative Narrative changes the tune for clients with ADHD and for those who suffer along with them. Taking a break from the noisy inner critic rests an overworked, overactive ADHD brain. Adding insights into what goes right and what IS right really opens capacity to find the "even better if…" options for dealing with people, deadlines, and goals. Narrative helps in many unusual ways. Lists, calendars, and agendas are lost less, and inner direction is used more. Giving people opportunities to use narrative has an unusual benefit. It helps them reorder their relationship with time, and timeliness. As Nikki put it, time is no longer a devouring monster, but rather a trusted assistant.

Chapter 6
GRATITUDE

It is good to give thanks

The next challenge for TimeSavor coaching clients, most especially for one "Janice," was to give voice to gratitude. As it turns out, Jack, Nikki, Gabe, Janice, and many others, were coming from places of great frustration, blame of others, and anger.

When Janice was asked if there were anyone in her life, past or present, she felt moved to thank, she answered, "No one. No one did right by me." This looked to be a coaching conversation stopper. If all there was to gratitude was giving someone else thanks, Janice made a good point. She didn't owe anyone. No one at all gave her justice and adequate care, and that's just the way it was. Yet was there perhaps even one exception to Janice's rule of "no thanks"? As time went on, Janice's readiness to explore that possibility did, in fact, lead to one small affirmative answer. Yet that small answer made a big difference for Janice.

From a Positive Psychology coaching perspective, why is it good to give thanks? What are the health benefits? What aspects of Positive Psychology coaching does gratitude support? Robert Biswas-Diener answers this in <u>Practicing Positive Psychology Coaching</u> (2010). He summarizes gratitude studies, whose results suggest higher levels of social support and lower levels of social anxiety related to gratitude practices. Low levels of social support and high levels of social anxiety are significant issues for those with ADHD, and this finding is an avenue for coaching support.

Additional studies suggest that building the strength of gratitude increases happiness and decreases depression. According to Bob Emmons, professor at the University of California, Davis, in his book, <u>Thanks!</u> (2007), "Gratitude" is the experience of recalling what goes right, connecting to something greater than one's self, having more positive emotions, and improved capacity to deal with adversity. It seems that those who can focus on what they have and on what goes right, even in situations as difficult as combat, are better able to access positive emotions, a clearer perspective, and a situational view open to positive options.

Gratitude is more than an emotion, which, when practiced and developed, has been shown to increase consistently our basic state of happiness, called our "set point." Practicing gratitude has also been shown to improve our sleep, and increase our energy. ADHD clients look for assistance in these two areas, as many report sleep disruption at night and ensuing fatigue during the day. Emmons describes gratitude as having two essential stages. These stages consist of "recognizing" and "acknowledging " (2007, pp. 3-5). Recognizing is an awakening. Recognizing may sound like: "Something good DID happen." "Something good is happening RIGHT NOW." "There really IS a strong possibility that something good is about to happen." Acknowledging is personal engagement. The good that came generously and unbidden is enhanced in its beneficial effect by the choice to respond with appreciation. Acknowledging may sound like: "Yes, I can see that this is good. Now, I lift my heart and voice in thanks."

"No one did right by me," kept Janice in an unhealthy and perpetually suspicious stance. Yet, she was at the same time very unhappy about her negativity. After some soul-searching, she took a chance at hunting for something that could merit even a particle of gratitude. Thus, Janice worked at recognizing something good that came her way from a source outside herself. For her, it was recognizing the gift of loyalty on the part of one solitary relative. She never even recognized that this kindness had come her way until she was challenged by the gratitude exercise.

Janice explained that there was a particular period of her life during which she made some significantly risky choices. She had harmed others by her impulsivity, and was called on it. Yet, this lone relative remained at Janice's side. From Janice's unchallenged perspective, this period in her life was all about slights and rejection. Her recollection was about being insulted, judged, and rejected by everybody in her entire universe. But that was not reality. Looking through the lens of gratitude, Janice discovered that one person had, in fact, remained her steadfast ally, offering unconditional love.

Janice was ready to acknowledge that she had greatly benefited from this constancy. She tried to express to her relative how much that fidelity meant. She wrote. The letter flowed easily, as did the tears. Janice was able to bring her gratitude letter to her relative. She experienced an unexpected boost in mood. A sense of gratitude was not a burden or obligation, she discovered. It was a warm feeling, and a relief. Someone did right by her.

Gratitude has a very strong and consistent relationship with increased happiness. Summarizing recent research on gratitude, the Harvard Medical School's Positive Psychology Special Health Report (Harvard Health Publications, 2009), underscored an increased capacity to deal with adversity (p.16). Recalling events that have brought about a grateful heart actually creates a somewhat optimistic mindset in times of trouble. Some people enduring adversity have a measure of hope that, since good things have happened before, they surely might happen yet again. They look for solutions to their problems and become active in helping themselves.

How do these areas in particular help coaching clients with ADHD-related time issues? Barbara Fredrickson, in <u>Positivity</u> (2009), discusses the evolutionary benefits of her "broaden and build" theory. When the brain is free of its powerful "fight/flight" response, it is able to broaden its understanding of the world as it is and of how it might be made better. It also allows for building of intellectual and emotional capacity. Practicing gratitude does precisely this.

Likewise, gratitude exercises permit clients with ADHD to release their negative narratives. With effort and patience, these clients are able to broaden their worldview to include what goes right. They also build upon realized and unrealized strengths to achieve deeply held goals, such as those related to improved time management.

Like a domino effect, increased happiness quiets the inner critic and then makes room for strengths awareness. Strengths awareness, then, leads to the use of strengths in managing choices, sticking to projects, and meeting goals that are desirable. Then, as gratitude increases, clients see themselves as a part of, rather than apart from, other people. "Other people matter" is at the heart of Positive Psychology, says Chris Peterson. Practicing gratitude is also known to improve overall health. Better overall health leads to better brain health. Detoxifying the body of harmful substances builds overall health, but more importantly, takes some stress off an overworked ADHD-type brain.

Bob Emmons' considerable research on the strength of gratitude suggested long-term benefits. Study participants felt optimistic and happy about their lives. They also exercised more and had fewer medical visits and illness. Certainly, improvements in base-line happiness and an increase in life satisfaction are essential to all coaching clients, especially those acutely dissatisfied with ADHD-related failures in life.

Another way gratitude can specifically benefit clients with ADHD is that it helps them create focus. Loss of focus is one of the major causes of time gaps and failure to follow through. The focus of gratitude is to appreciate what you <u>have</u>, rather than nursing grudges about what you don't have. While ADHD clients don't have thinking processes identical to most other people, they <u>do</u> have thinking processes that can be celebrated and appreciated. Becoming grateful for what you have, what you've been given freely, and what can contribute to satisfaction, creates a new baseline of happiness, as well as an all-important positive inner narrative.

Strategies for Gratitude

Gratitude exercises are an important element in Positive Psychology coaching. The following are exercises famously used by Martin Seligman, by Bob Emmons, and in further studies by Sonja Lyubomirsky, among others.

<u>The Gratitude Visit (and The Gratitude Letter)</u>—Martin Seligman, as previously mentioned, assigned study participants to write and deliver a gratitude letter to someone they had never properly thanked. A review of participants' scores revealed that their levels of happiness increased significantly, while their levels of depression decreased at the same time. The effects were lasting, with participants showing benefits even a month afterward. Subsequent studies have used the gratitude letter writing process, but suggest that the letter need not be sent or delivered to have the same impact on positivity and connectedness as in the original assignment.

When Gabe agreed to write a gratitude letter, he felt a bit hesitant and sheepish. After all, Gabe is a man of few words. Writing is not usually an activity he associates with the "flow" state. Walking silently through the woods with his hunting dog is more Gabe's style. Yet, within moments, something clicked for him. He said, "I know who to write a gratitude letter to: my wife. She's my best friend." Things got very quiet on Gabe's end of the conversation at that point.

At the next coaching session, Gabe reported that the gratitude letter had meant so much to both of them. His voice had a softness that had been absent until that point. He talked about the warmth in his heart as he thought about Sue's reaction to the letter. She had never imagined the depth of gratitude he felt for her. When he recounted the details of his ADHD struggles and her supportive response, both of them became emotional. Gabe had been the object of ridicule by some family members. Sue witnessed it all, and brought Gabe comfort and reassurance. He had never before thanked her, as his anger and shame had ruled the day. What surprised Gabe very much was, his bitter feelings diminished as he reached inside to thank Sue. Best of all, when Gabe returned from a long day's work the next evening, Sue surprised him with an incredible meal of her "signature" homemade vegetable lasagna, which just happened to be his favorite!

Gratitude Journal—Study participants wrote in their journals once a week. They were to focus on five things they were grateful for during the week. The participants wrote during a 10-week period in Emmons' study, and described positive emotions continuing for some time after their journaling was finished.

TimeSavor Coaching clients used Heidi Grant Halvorson's (2010) system of "if…then," as previously discussed, to establish a firm commitment to journaling. "Allen," for example, decided to write in his journal each day for a week. He designed the following success motivator based on Halvorson's work that went like this: "If it's 10:00 pm, then, I'll write five things I'm grateful for today in my journal, while sitting at my desk in my bedroom." This particular gratitude exercise had a very powerful positive effect on client Allen and his son, "Anthony."

Allen struggled with ADHD for his entire life. He couldn't work for someone else, so he developed his own practice in the field of finance. He had flexible hours, worked from home, had total control over his workspace, and often wandered his property while on the phone with clients. That aspect of his life brought Allen many rewards. Life with Anthony, at the moment, did not seem as rewarding. As Allen said, it was a nightmare.

Anthony also had an ADHD diagnosis. A series of difficult circumstances, including abandonment by his mother, left him in the sole care of Allen. As Anthony entered adolescence with a vengeance, Allen was at a loss. Their relationship was at the mercy of their distinct and conflicting ADHD behaviors. Effective communication became the early victim of impulsivity, lack of self-regulation, and failure to read interpersonal cues. Approaching desperation, Allen became willing to try a gratitude journal, not just once a week, but rather every day for one week.

His days became richer with appreciation, and he found he took fewer of life's benefits for granted. However, nowhere in that first week's journaling did Anthony's name show up! Allen's challenge for the following week was to include his gratitude for things about Anthony that were currently in disguise.

Anthony was arrested during that week for vandalism. He had to appear, at a later date, in court. Allen demanded that Anthony make restitution. Anthony dug in and refused.

That incident was still fresh in Allen's memory, when Anthony took the keys to the car and had a joy ride with friends. Also during that same week, Anthony "accidentally" damaged his father's laptop, the one that had just come back from the repair shop. He sulked for the remainder of the week. He was being completely misunderstood. Allen was a terrible father who never listened. Anthony protested loudly that he was unfairly treated, what with curfews and loss of privileges. What a challenge for Allen! Allen argued back, point by point, loudly. Both dug in. Communication ceased.

Yet Allen wrote in his gratitude journal every day during that long week. The first thing he was grateful for was Anthony's beautiful head of hair! That was it for the first entry. In the following entries, Allen wrote that he was grateful that Anthony had fully recovered from a devastating childhood illness. He was grateful Anthony was alive. He was well enough to get into trouble. He was healthy enough to be annoying. He was growing tall and strong. He had the mental and physical ability to take the keys and drive a car! That's when everything began to shift.

Allen decided he was not going to remain in a contest of wills with Anthony. He settled peacefully into the confident role of the head of the house. He realized that the love he felt for that sick little boy had vanished, mainly because Anthony was a teenage boy with self-destructive ADHD impulsivity and oppositional behaviors. And so, Allen became grateful all over again that his son had life and health and a chance at better days. Things could be so much worse, thought Allen. "Where there's life, there's hope," became his new slogan. The father's love, like Anthony himself, was alive.

Amazingly, Allen approached Anthony and asked if they could sit together so that Allen could listen to whatever Anthony needed to say. He promised to just listen and not jump in with platitudes and judgments. Anthony was reluctant and suspicious. When he at first declined to talk, Allen backed off. He tried again. This time, Allen shared a little story from his own ADHD-influenced adolescent behavior. The story seemed to "prime the pump" for Anthony. The warming of the relationship did not occur overnight, but it did occur. Some days later, Anthony spoke, and Allen just listened with an understanding and grateful heart.

Three Good Things—Sonja Lyubomirsky worked with participants on writing down three good things that happened during the day. Most participants reported a boost in mood. What Lyubomirsky also discovered was that the benefits of this exercise are very dependent upon the participants' preferences for how often they journal and how many good things they prefer to include.

Lucy knew she had much for which she was grateful. But, she said, her thoughts were like butterflies and her net had a big hole in it. Appreciation for her current state of affairs slipped right out that hole. She desired to have a more organized life, but couldn't imagine how spending time on recounting three good things each evening for a week could help. The burdens on her mind made her frantic, especially when she tried to retire for the night. That's when the worst of it happened for Lucy. She would wander the house seeking respite, and then fall asleep in some awkward position somewhere in the living room or kitchen. Fatigue trapped her mind and filled her days with forgetfulness and mistakes. She wondered aloud, then, if Three Good Things actually could help.

A chart from the Harvard Health Report on Positive Psychology (2009) appealed to Lucy. First of all, it listed the days of the week down the left hand column. This would prompt Lucy to consider each day as an opportunity to be grateful. It was an organizing and memory tool, and Lucy had a real fondness for graphic organizers!

Next, in the column headers across the top of the chart, Lucy found areas of life written out to prompt her thoughts. On the chart, each day's Three Good Things could fit within five column headings: Work, Family or Friends, Nature, Uplifting Experiences, and Material Comforts. This really clicked with Lucy. As she often did, she translated her coaching homework into a calming bedtime routine for her little boys. The boys would get very quiet and think hard about the three good things of the day. They could share aloud or keep it in the quiet of their hearts. One morning, Lucy found that her artistic little boys had drawn pictures of the things they were grateful for, and had posted them on their "art wall"!

Recording the Three Good Things in her chart did not help Lucy fall peacefully asleep every night, but it did improve the boy's bedtime routine! And, while Lucy spent her own quiet moment moving aside the troubles of the day, she did find her mind ease up as she let appreciation for the day's good things enter in.

Some TimeSavor Coaching Narrative Exercises

"Downward Comparison: Great moments out of bad moments"—This is an interesting, stretching exercise for some clients who like a little variety with their gratitude writing. It requires clients to go deeper, seeking the silver lining in an otherwise unpleasant moment. In their Positive Psychology research in the field of trauma, cited in <u>Trauma, Growth and Recovery</u>, (Joseph & Linley, 2007) psychologists Alex Linley and Stephen

Joseph call this psychological strength of resilience "benefit finding." Downward comparisons are stories about how things could have been worse. Guiding benefit-finding questions ask, "What strength did you use to meet this adversity?" "What did you learn about yourself from this experience?" This exercise is not for everyone, but it really worked for Janice.

Since "no one ever did right by her," Janice found gratitude very antithetical to her life. In great part, she came to coaching for help managing time related issues. These "temporal" problems included keeping to a schedule, being on time for appointments with clients, and developing consistent practices of follow-up. In addition, she revealed early on that she didn't always have the best relationships with others.

One of her most traumatic relationships was with her previous boss, who had supervised her in another department, but within the same company and office space. She could, she explained, potentially run into this woman at any time on any day. This kept Janice perpetually preoccupied with fear of conflict. It was little wonder that she had become avoidant of stepping out of her work area to meet with clients and follow up with them!

Janice liked the "bad moments" part of this exercise all too well. However, discovering the "great moments" was challenging. Some follow-up questions got her started thinking. How, for example, had she found a way to improve her situation? What had she done to survive? What had she learned about herself? What did she get from this experience?

With those prompts, Janice was able to pivot away from her negativity and fear. She told a story of the strengths of wisdom, resilience, and courage. Wisdom came with Janice's diagnosis of ADHD, which she received while she was working for this supervisor. Janice began to realize that the very things she was excoriated for by her boss were related to her neurological condition. She tried to explain this, but received ridicule for her efforts. Using the strength of wisdom, Janice began looking for a change that would save her health and mind.

She undertook the process of finding another position within her company. This took tremendous resilience in the face of company politics. She persevered despite obstacles and setbacks. She continued to endure the emotional hardships of her untenable situation, with the hope that it would soon be over. With great courage, she put herself out there, asking for a transfer, and risking repercussions from her supervisor. Finally, she found another manager who was willing to take her on under these less than ideal circumstances.

Janice was ready to try the "great moments" part of this exercise. Her first words of gratitude were these: "I am grateful to my former boss for the opportunity to grow. If it hadn't been for her, I never would have sought out this great, new position with one of the few managers in the company who 'gets it' about ADHD. "

She went on to write about her gratitude to her new boss. In the traumatic aftermath of leaving her previous position, Janice had missed the reality of this person's kindness toward her. In fact, she completely missed what courage it took for her new boss to take her on. She was grateful, truly.

Janice also learned that she herself was a person who "did right by Janice." She felt wise, resilient, and courageous. She added three new descriptors to her own self-talk. And this helped tremendously when she worked with clients.

"The Gratitude Letter: The Heroes in Your Heart"—This is a version of the familiar gratitude letter. This one is not delivered or sent, however. It's written to someone clients hold in their hearts as a model of desirable strengths, and whose lives have deeply moved them. The interesting twist on this exercise is that clients are asked to imagine the sound of this person's voice while writing. Engaging this process, called polyvocality, has the effect of bringing to the writer a deeper and more immediate dimension of the "hero's" wisdom, along with other modeled strengths. The "voice" of the hero becomes part of a repertoire of sustainable emotional supports

In fact, Ryan Niemiec, positive psychologist, author, and speaker, noted recently that coaches are very familiar with polyvocality, but from a negative side. It is best known to coaching clients as the various voices of inner critics (2011). Introducing the countering and protective voices of the heroes of the heart creates an opportunity for clients to find wisdom to lean on and internalize. It has a detoxifying effect. It also has an elevating effect, creating opportunities for clients to literally "lift up their hearts."

Is it good to for people to "lift up their hearts"? Wonderful research on this topic is being published and developed. Scientists, notably Barb Fredrickson, University of North Carolina, Chapel Hill, and Richard Davidson, University of Wisconsin, Madison, and suggest the importance of vagus nerve "tone," a marker of optimism and well-being. The vagus nerve extends from within the brain stem, traveling to the heart. Its very important job is to connect the brain to the visceral organs. In so doing, it acts to regulate emotions and bodily systems. The effectiveness of the vagus nerve is measured by its tone, or fitness, according to Fredrickson and Davidson. The higher the vagal tone, the better the vagus nerve performs at regulating emotions and body systems. High vagal tone is related to both a person's physical health and the ability to feel loving connections with others, and has been shown to improve with simple loving kindness mediation. It is possible to improve vagal nerve tone, and thus improve the regulatory pathways connecting the head, heart, and vital organs. Improvements in vagal tone are related to good health, focus, and emotional balance. (Fredrickson & Davidson, 2011).

Since bringing forth loving connections is a way to regulate emotions and focus, contemplating the heroes of the heart in this exercise, links to these benefits. The novelty of this exercise, plus attainable attentional benefits, are attractive to many ADHD clients seeking a variety of "exercise equipment" to build related time management strengths.

In trying to bring forward the heroes of her heart, Nikki recalled both of her grandmothers. She, however, chose to write about the one she had spent the least amount of time with. She became curious about this woman, whose difficult life as an immigrant ultimately led to her early death. Nikki began to look further into this ancestor's life history.

She found the story of an adventurer who left the familiarity of her hometown to travel across the ocean for a better life. Her grandmother was a bit of a rebel and didn't always do what was expected of a woman of her day. She broke with strongly held tradition and entered into a mixed-faith marriage. To start anew, she and her young husband immigrated to America, settling in an Eastern city. There, she used skills from her former life to make the unfamiliar feel like home. She became an urban gardener, providing her family with inexpensive yet nutritious foods. From the lessons of her previous life, she made certain nothing went to waste.

Nikki, then, wrote of this woman who showed loyalty to her loved ones, fiercely supporting them with her hard work and wise sayings. She wrote also of a woman who, with no formal training, had the instincts and skill of a nurse, who offered her help to neighbors and friends in times of sickness and trouble. The hero of her heart, Nikki wrote, shared a powerful genetic connection. "We share DNA," she wrote, "and much more." And they shared strengths of loving kindness, curiosity, wisdom, and courage as well. And what were the words Nikki "heard" from her grandmother? "Nikki, I did it. If I can do it, you can do it, too."

As a tangible reminder, Nikki carries with her a cracked and faded black-and-white photo of her grandmother's original kitchen garden. The garden itself looks to be about the size of a postage stamp. It is Nikki's imagination that adds three dimensions, color, and fragrance to the little snapshot. Nikki knows the name of every perennial and annual she sees there, of every herb and botanical, edible and decorative, arranged in tight little rows, like ribbons on a hero's chest. She looks at the photo, or simply slips her hand into her pocket to touch it. It provides her, she says, with the feeling of unconditional love when she really needs it, and of the sound of her grandmother's voice saying, "Nikki...you can do it, too."

"What Worked Well Today? How Did You Help?"—Nathan desired more positivity in his life. He felt those around him communicated exclusively their disappointment to him. He found it difficult to lift his spirits up enough to engage in standard gratitude exercises. He was willing to give "What Worked Well Today" a try. He sat down at bedtime and practiced a moment of quiet reflection. "What did go well today?" To his amazement, Nathan learned that his life was more than just a string of moments marked with failure. He noticed things like being on time for class. He noticed things like remembering to call his mother when he said he would. He found that he could stop and notice the times during the day when he was able to use his top strengths. Nathan was a convert. He began to project an improved attitude to those around him.

He took the exercise to the next important step and asked the follow-up question: "What did I do to help make this good thing happen today?" Nathan realized that the coaching work he was doing was changing his mindset. Ironically, he realized that his fixed mindset was perpetuating the negative opinions of others. It was all about a self-fulfilling prophecy. Nathan recognized this unhelpful attitude: "They all think I'm a failure anyhow. They always say I can't stick with anything. Well, I'll show them. I'll be a failure and dabble with a million things at once and never finish any of them!"

He practiced this gratitude exercise for several weeks, acknowledging that good things truly did happen every day, and that he actually played a role in making them happen. He became genuinely grateful for the times things worked out well. Nathan began to assume a growth mindset, and soon stopped trying to prove his critics right. He stopped trying to prove them wrong, too. It was enough for him that he had taken off his blinders and could find a spark of happiness in things that went well.

Why is it good to give thanks? Positive Psychology researchers have tested and validated several benefits that directly assist ADHD clients. Where clients feel social isolation and alienation related to their differences, gratitude practices serve to connect them with what goes right and with social support. Research strongly suggests gratitude practices decrease social anxiety, a significant up-building gain for clients with ADHD.

Participants in gratitude studies showed greater health benefits that lasted over time. They were less likely to miss class or work due to illness or injury. Their levels of happiness increased, while their levels of depression decreased. Gratitude is recalling what goes right, connecting to something greater than one's self, experiencing more positive emotions, and improving one's capacity to deal with adversity.

For a person with ADHD, these benefits broaden sustainable efforts in time management areas. Promptness, keeping commitments, goal management, and work completion are all time sensitive areas that cause problems. For those with ADHD, strengthening bonds with others, and with their own better qualities, builds capacity for respect and empathy. Time management gets better for clients along with a frequently practiced awareness that "other people matter," a classic summary of what Positive Psychology is about.

Chapter 7
SAVORING

Taste and see

"Savoring" is consciously enjoying the good things and pleasures of life. Savoring has a present-centeredness, appreciating the moment as it unfolds. In this regard, savoring is considered one of the time management strengths, within the virtues listed by Peterson and Seligman in <u>Character Strengths and Virtues: A Handbook and Classification</u>, (2004). The Harvard Medical School's <u>Positive Psychology Special Health Report</u> (2009) suggests that appreciating the big and small moments in life builds happiness. This is in contrast to the negativity and unhappiness experieced by many clients with ADHD. They often reach for a kind of conformity and thought process that belongs to others, but not to them. As they learn to savor what they have, rather than agitate over what they are lacking, an openness to greater contentment comes along.

The work of researchers Fred Bryant, of Loyola University Chicago, and Joseph Veroff, of the University of Michigan, has as its focus the Positive Psychology strength of Savoring. In their book, <u>Savoring: A New Model of Positive Experience</u> (2007), Bryant and Veroff define the "temporal" properties of savoring as being those of positive reminiscence, appreciation of the present moment, and optimistic anticipation. Their research suggests that the beneficial effects of taking the time to manage time were enhanced and prolonged. This temporal magnification occurred when positive moments were shared with others, or were captured in some way, as in photos, paintings, journals, or mementos.

Research also suggests that savoring is helpful in creating positive models for making choices. For example, to simultaneously overwhelm the mind with multiple good options is to create confusion and loss of focus. This is often seen in ADHD thinking, when every option floods the conscious mind completely unfiltered. Not every good and novel choice is compatible with choices that need to be made for the sake of existing commitments. Two or more good options at the same time exacerbate the ADHD brain's tendency toward loss of focus. Savoring helps teach clients to step back and slow down, a very important aspect for effective decision-making.

The temporal properties of savoring are of particular interest to coaching clients with ADHD. Thinking in terms of past, present, and future, experienced in novel ways through savoring, supports coaching processes that reinforce sequencing and prioritizing. As Bryant and Veroff (2007) describe it, negative thoughts have the power to hijack attention, to the exclusion of other important areas of focus. People with ADHD can receive coaching help to reduce negativity, freeing up brain capacity, especially in areas of executive functioning. To aid in strengthening the power to focus, the authors suggest exercises that support three of the main functions of savoring, that is, prolonging the moment, intensifying the moment, and shifting gears toward appreciating the moment. Their research further suggests four main types of savoring processes, (pp. 138-139)

1. Thanksgiving—for gifts freely given
2. Marveling—awe
3. Basking—experiencing personal victory
4. Luxuriating—being absorbed in physical activities that promote restoration

In <u>Positivity</u> (2009), Barbara Fredrickson emphasizes the value of savoring as an antidote to negativity and as one of the factors containing what she has determined to be positivity's ten forms. They appear closely related to Bryant and Veroff's (2007) four main savoring processes listed above. Fredrickson's list includes "awe" and "thanksgiving," as does Bryant and Veroff's list. Fredrickson's forms of positivity add "amusement," along with "hope," "inspiration," "interest," "joy," "love," "pride," and "serenity." Fredrickson concludes that savoring, which can arise from a heartfelt experience of any of the ten forms of positivity, can broaden and build a person's capacity to think and achieve.

The nature of savoring relates to a positive point of view regarding time. Fredrickson encourages the experience of savoring in the past, present, and future orientations, the concept well established by Bryant and Veroff (2007). Building a positive relationship with time—past, present, and future—continues to work toward the "broaden and build" capacities of ADHD clients, as they seek the tools to advance good order, timeliness, empathy for the time constraints of others, and direct-line focus toward future goals.

Strategies for Savoring

<u>"Positive Reminiscence"</u>—Savoring the past is sometimes bittersweet for clients with ADHD. When a client is ready to do so, however, artifacts, souvenirs, and shared stories enhance the experience.

One of the first narrations encouraged by Appreciative Inquiry is to "tell about a time when you were at your best." This is one example of positive reminiscence. It is a particularly difficult one for clients with ADHD, whose past resembles a war zone, at least in the traumatic negativity they often describe. What happens when the negative story needs telling first?

Tatsuya Hirai, of the Ritsumeikan Asia Pacific University, and colleague Manami Ozaki, of the Sagami Women's University (Hirari, 2011), suggest using great gentleness in encouraging clients to narrate stories of their failure and shame. It does no good to rush to the positive side of reminiscence, they have found. In fact, by allowing them an airing of these negative stories, the strengths side of the client can be observed.

Tayyab Rashid, strengths researcher from the Values in Action Institute in Cincinnati, and the University of Toronto, confirms the findings of Hirai and Ozaki. Rashid warns that rushing a client into positive reminiscence can cause a very serious, if not permanent, breach in the coach-client relationship. Patience and readiness are more important than the Positive Psychology intervention, all three researchers affirm. Along these same lines, Harvard professor Tal Ben-Shahar, in his book Happier (2007), further explains that those people, like certain ADHD clients in the midst of serious sadness or loss, find it unhelpful to be asked to focus on the pursuit of happiness.

This is exactly the way positive reminiscence worked for many of the clients mentioned so far. The most notable story of "me at my best" came from one of the most traumatized clients: Nikki. She did have to give considerable voice to her shame and alienation, and to stories of exclusion from birthday parties, removal from family celebrations and school events, and to tales of hostility directed at her by classroom teachers.

One day, readiness prevailed, and Nikki had a powerful recollection of her truest and best self. She was three years old. From her father's arms, she could see the most amazing sight: a seemingly endless strand of beach. "I think my little feet were actually moving before he even put me down. And I ran. I ran and ran and ran with nothing to stop me. Nothing was in the way and there was no end to this feeling of exhilaration. I don't even remember stopping! But that was the best feeling I ever remember, running, and running and running. It was me at my best."

Now, Nikki can actualize the remembrance of that "at her best" feeling. It helps her decision making process when she is determining what to say "yes" to and what "no" comes along with that. Her touchstone is that running-baby feeling of freedom, safety, beauty of nature, kinesthetic gratification, and wonder. The "yes" that comes closest to those qualities, wins.

"Attention to the Present Moment"—This starts with a very simple mindfulness meditation used by novice meditation practitioners. The client gets comfortably seated and simply becomes intensely aware of the process of breathing, starting with the sensation of air entering into and passing out of, the nostrils. When attention wanders, the task is to simply return attention to breaths in and breaths out, as they pass through the nostrils.

For clients with ADHD, this is both a challenge and an enjoyable exercise in building mental muscles of clarity and focus. Practicing clearing the mind of judgment, affect, busy thoughts, and returning the mind to focus, builds the skill of attention, even in a brain that loves novelty more than most other brains. Why is this? Because the ADHD brain is also a very curious brain, and finds delight in the challenge of discovery and mastery. Mindfulness creates opportunities to find out what will happen next through concentration and return to focus. Over time, this practice plays a beneficial role, protecting the brain in times of chaotic stimulation.

A client, "Henry," was the stereotypical absent-minded professor. He was a successful artist and filmmaker who also taught advanced courses on the college level. He was beloved by his students, as much for his befuddlement as for his talent. Still, Henry was unhappy and wanted to make some changes.

The temporal demands of academic life were wearing him down. He was perpetually reprimanded by administration for failure to submit grades, syllabi, recommendations, and so on. He annoyed colleagues with irresponsible promises and unfulfilled commitments. He attended meetings days late or days early, but rarely on the scheduled date. He stumbled into sessions with arms filled with loose papers, art supplies, and video equipment. Henry was a sight: salt-and-pepper hair in wiry spikes, glasses slipping, and clothes smudged with paints. He wanted a little less turmoil without too much sacrifice.

Henry was the loving father of six energetic, creative children. When several of his youngsters began having attentional difficulties in the classroom, school officials recommended testing. Testing produced the diagnosis of ADHD. Henry's wife suspected this was, to a great degree, a description of Henry. She suggested to Henry that he get tested as well. For several years, she suggested this to Henry. His children began to graduate. Ten years went by. Still, his wife suggested testing for ADHD to Henry. When Henry was sufficiently miserable and embarrassed by his colleagues' hostility, he went for testing, and brought home an ADHD diagnosis to his wife.

Overwhelmed and outnumbered, she pressed Henry to "do something" about his new ADHD diagnosis. This time, Henry didn't wait a decade. Along with therapy and medication, Henry's doctor strongly advised working regularly with an ADHD coach.

Henry's lovely artistic self readily took to practicing appreciation of the present moment. Oh, the blissful white quiet inside his head. Yes, he would get distracted from concentrating on his breaths many, many times at each attempt. However, returning to attention was not so violent, not so disruptive, that he couldn't do it. After much practice attending to the present moment, Henry declared with great joy: "The future stays out there!" What a wonderful description of freedom from distractibility!

Henry hasn't changed in ways that are important to him. Henry says, "There's always room for improvement!" But he is less likely to over-commit now. He is more likely to attend meetings exactly when they are scheduled. He has become willing to travel within the hallowed halls pushing a rolling supply cart, thus keeping his supplies and equipment much better contained. Also on that cart is a bulging folio subduing Henry's numerous files. As for paint-spattered clothes, there is unlikely to be a change in that regard, although now, Henry DOES change his outfits more frequently than once a decade.

"Optimistic Anticipation"—Henry was finally freed from the tyranny of the future. Yet, "savoring" invited him, and the other coaching clients, to enter into contemplation of the future, this time with optimistic anticipation. Henry was reassured that the future stays out there when you can learn to preview it while looking through the lens of your strengths.

Predicting future outcomes with optimism is quite different from that familiar sigh of resignation that everything will turn out poorly. Coaching clients with ADHD at first tentatively "try on" the idea that it IS possible to approach the future with confidence, by rehearsing situations to come. A good place to start is using narratives like "My Best Possible Self" and "My Best Possible Future." In order to discover potential obstacles, the exercise, "A Story With Two Endings" can help.

Another tool for optimistic anticipation is leaning on positive experiences from the past that help to inform similar strategies for the up-coming situation. It is also extremely helpful for clients to offer themselves something to look forward to as they take action toward their goals. They can choose from a richer menu of things they savor, past and present, and offer themselves such a reward in the future. All this is called "planning," a sometimes-neglected strategy for many coaching clients.

In Do More Great Work, Michael Bungay Stanier (2010, pp. 111-142) offers readers many "maps" to use in planning for optimistic future outcomes. "What's Possible?" is the heading for one of Bungay Stanier's maps that has been very helpful to many clients. The names designating this map's list sections follow the concepts of tapping into what you already know and adding things you actually enjoy. First, clients list things they've already been considering under a heading called, "The ideas you already have." Then, clients choose an idea and make its completion a goal. Next, they decide how to categorize the various tasks necessary reach this goal. Finally, they place these tasks into categories such as "Easy to Do," "Fun to Do," "Fast to Do," "Brave to Do," and "Provocative to Do." TimeSavor coaching clients use this map for help with anticipating a good outcome. It has become for many of them a filter for free-floating future demands and opportunities.

There are many ways to enter into a savoring state of mind, but one of them has to do with being more present to the present moment. This is very important because so many clients with ADHD rush to keep up with their thoughts, yet ironically fall behind the more their thoughts race. In coaching sessions, they share images of their minds to help express this feeling. Some liken the way their minds look to that of a cluttered desktop, or an overflowing laundry hamper, to piles of unopened mail and past-due bills, or an impassable room with mountains of clutter.

The prevalence of these well-habituated images is a constant source of stress hormones released in the brain. Too much time spent in fight/flight mode, as in the life or death hunt of the lion and its prey, suppresses neural pathways to the prefrontal cortex, the thinking-planning-reflecting-time management area of the brain. Unrelenting stress also impedes the functioning of the hippocampus, a brain structure involved with emotions and with long- and short-term memory. So says Stanford University biologist Robert M. Sapolsky in his enjoyable book, Why Zebras Don't Get Ulcers (1998).

Stress hormones, such as glucocorticoids, can suppress higher order thinking skills, like planning and time management. They are also known to have serious health consequences on various organ systems and joints. How does savoring help? It provides clients with a much needed break from pressured thinking and allows for a beneficial shift from stress hormones to those related to calm and pleasure, such as serotonin, oxytocin, and dopamine (Fredrickson & Davidson, 2011).

Some TimeSavor Coaching Savoring Exercises

"Once, A Small Good Thing Happened To Me On My Way To My Future"—This exercise teaches clients to be mindful of the little things that went well along the way, but went unrecognized. Clients build more positive and fulfilling relationship between the good things that happened in their near- and distant past, that are manifest in present day successes. Then, clients identify an aspect of their current lives that works well for them that is, one that they savor. They recognize a character strength that is related to this positive aspect of their present time. The client commences a backward journey of positive reminiscence to discover what small, good thing in the past was key to the positive future. Clients often find that there is a single relatively obscure moment, or a brief encounter that really influenced them at their best. Then they allow feelings of pleasure and awe to enter in, appreciative for the small good thing that came their way.

For Tom, the unlikely good thing was being drafted. In the service, he learned about airplanes. He loved them. The discipline of the army carried through to some big moves for Tom in civilian life. Tom took a direct path to an industry associated with jet flyers. So Tom stopped for a moment of pleasant remembrance for a small, good encounter with flight engineering while in the service.

"A Cup of Tea Tastes Good"—When is a cup of tea not a cup of tea? When it tastes good. Then, it is an event that engenders savoring. As Hallowell and Ratey observe in Delivered from Distraction (2006), some clients with ADHD have spent so much time with feelings of sadness and loss, they have a difficult time lifting out of a depressive state to feel momentary pleasure and enjoyment. This state of "anhedonia" is the opposite side of Positive Psychology's view of the "hedonic state" of relative happiness and wellbeing, and the "eudaemonic state," describing a contentment that arises from having meaning and relatedness.

"First Time/Last Time"—In "Noticing" exercises, clients are invited to regard the ordinary as if it is the first time they ever experienced it. One very stressed and sad client remarked that drinking tea throughout the day had become simply an exercise is swallowing hot fluid with a slight hint of color. Tea slipped past all taste buds and even remained out of her field of vision. And then she noticed one day, quite spontaneously, that it actually tasted good. She found that her thinking slowed down in a most pleasurable way as she engaged many more of her senses in enjoyment of the brew, pretending to herself it was the first time she had ever experienced drinking tea.

Another side of this exercise is for clients to try and imagine that this will be the last time for a very long time that they will get to enjoy a cup of tea. Imagine what that might be like. Savoring has the effect to increase happiness by expanding and enhancing pleasurable experiences, as Seligman suggests in Flourish (2011). This aspect of the savoring exercise sets the client up for desiring the experience does not come quickly to its end. Prolonged enjoyment, hightening the senses, concentrating on retaining the desirability of sipping the tea, are incredibly powerful vehicles for improving clients' relationship with time. With savoring, then, time becomes a partner in pleasure and happiness.

Temporal experience markers offer "alert" signals to those willing to savor more of life's moments. A "savoring alert" may come with the desire to relive again and again a moment filled with powerful uplifting experiences, like the birth of a child, memories of travel highpoints, or what it was like to reach a difficult goal. A savoring alert, as seen above, may also be recognized in the desire that a special moment never end, as in viewing a natural wonder, coming to the end of an awe-inspiring yet potentially unrepeatable experience, or in the way it feels to be on the threshold of saying goodbye to a loved one.

Many people with ADHD have as one of their strengths, the gift of curiosity. At times, it is a pathway to distractibility and unproductive hyperfocus. However, Todd Kashdan, clinical psychologist and psychology professor at George Mason University, has studied this strength extensively, and has written Curious? Discover the Missing Ingredient to a Fulfilling Life (2009).

Kashdan writes about a topic related to savoring, that is, creating lasting interests and passions. Adding to our understanding of enhancing and extending pleasurable moments, he notes that our curious moments may be brief, but they do have the effect of creating overflowing interest and excitement that boost our moods.

Clients can develop "curiosity alerts" in the same way they can experience savoring alerts. From this increase in self-awareness, curiosity can be developed to create memory links to those things clients find to be of value and important in their lives. Creating these neural links is a very helpful way to assist the memory functions of ADHD brains, and the power of linking sets of knowledge to pleasurable experienes should be used often, and, never underestimated. Kashdan (2009) confirms through his studies that drawing connections starts during those moments that are so interesting, and so feed our curiosity, that we wish they would never end. The power of the mind to focus, then, is known to be a highly desirable trait sought after by clients with ADHD. Kashdan's work (2009) strongly suggests that focus can be developed through curiosity's tendancy to become an enduring interest when linked to personal meaning, values, and accomplishments.

"Where Did This Come From?"—This savoring exercise is also related to the strength of curiosity. Further, it is supported by the ADHD brain's attraction to novelty, as well as its ability to hyperfocus. In fact, it can even be considered a mini-vacation, allowing the ADHD brain to do what it likes to do best.

Clients are encouraged to slow down and savor an experience, such as sipping a cup of tea. Then, they allow their curiosity and imagination to take them on a journey backward in time, as far back as their interest, and availability to do so will allow, toward the beginning of the all the many processes and people that got the tea from the soil into their cups.

For example, client "Larry" is quite a brilliant fellow whose top strengths include cuiosity and love of learning. He is so curios, however, that he rarely finishes any of his wonderful projects. He is a very good writer, but a great deal of his work remains unfinished. So, Larry readily took to this exercise of Where Did This Come From? very naturally. He allowed himself mini-vacations along the lines of his interest in whole and organic foods. For example, he would ponder something as exotic as a pomegranite. He would let his mind go backward, step by step, from the check out clerk at the market, to the produce clerk, to the transport of the fruit from the port to the market, from the local truck to the port, from the local truck to the grove, from the grove to the farmer, and so on. He made up stories for each leg of his journey backward. His stories were free flowing and without pressure. They were lovely intervals of stream of consciousness. Larry didn't do this exercise for any other purpose than that he enjoyed it, and was quite good at it.

But, this exercise had unintended benefits. Typically a socially withdrawn man, Larry found an opportunity to be very engaging and amusing among fellow group members of a civic organization. At a recent dinner sponsored by the group, Larry unintentionally engaged his dinner companions in a brainstorming game of "Where Did This Come From?" He enjoyed their delight and engagement, and realized this helped him get more practice at being socially comfortable. That was one unintended benefits, but there were more.

Larry the Where-Did-This-Come-From storyteller became Larry the Storyteller-Who-Finished-Writing-Something. His personalized ADHD "brain vacations" did two unexpected things beyond increasing the ability to savor. First, Larry got very interested in the production, transport, and benefits of whole organic foods. Next, his other in-progress writing attempts flowed more easily. The result was, Larry achieved the desire of his heart, which was to create a useful and desirable on-line information product. And this he did, finishing the project by creating a popular subscription newsletter promoting plant based diets.

"Take A Photo"—Sonja Lyubomirsky (2007) has noted how much the actual act of looking through a lens and snapping a photo can enhance savoring. TimeSavor clients have enjoyed trying this, taking novel shots, close up shots, and broad vista shots. They have increased their ability to deeply concentrate, and allow Signature Strengths of appreciation of beauty and transcendance to enhance the pleasurable savoring (Peterson & Seligman, Character Strengths and Virtues: A Handbook and Classification, 2004). The idea here is to create a view that can make the ordinary extraordinary. By creating their own novel and provocative points of view, clients have experienced through photography a mood boost along with a boost in concentration. Most importantly, this exercise, that is framing the ordinary into the extraordinary, has aided clients with their practice of savoring.

For example, Jack the pilot has had many wonderful opportunities, soaring through the clouds to take almost surrealistic photos that have elevated his spirits and captured an experience he can share with other appreciative viewers. Certainly Henry, a videographer, has really spread the savoring message through experimentation with digital still photos and black and white techniques. His favorite subject: random shots of people. Larry, through this exercise, has found that he has quite an eye for composition. He is very nearly ready to take action and join a photography club, another effort to increase social competence.

His ability to savor a moment in time has grown along with his skill as a photographer. He loves to create out-of-the-ordinary compositions of familiar historic sites. Lucy and Nikki have learned to use the fingers on both their hands to create a virtual lens. They hold the shot in their own minds' eyes and savor it through meditating on the tiniest details held within their "frame." This works well, too, especially for those clients who are inspired by an unusal element, but have forgotten their cameras!

This "Take A Photo" exercise has also inspired clients to change up their ordinary routines, to take different routes, to make different stops along the way. This novelty and break with routine is something that both Lyubomirsky (2007) and Fredrickson (2009) have recognized as a way to happiness.

"Take A Photo" is amazingly helpful when it fits the client, but is a complete non-starter when it is a poor fit. Although both clients Janice and Gabe would like to savor more, linger with pleasurable moments, and boost their happiness, "Take A Photo" has not been successful for them. Their path to happiness and well being will proceed along a different route. Fortunately, Janice, Gabe and the other TimeSavor clients have a repertoire of exercises to keep things fresh and fit their needs as the situation requires.

"Here's Something I Look Forward To"—To help clients stay the course on longer term tasks, it helps to offer something to their dopamine receptors to keep their neurological pleasure and reward centers from overwhelming their best resolves. To write about things they look forward to, helps clients to develop what can become a repertoire for self-motivation. Clients are asked to think of something they look forward to at the end of the day, and to deliberate think of something that will bring them some comfort and enjoyment each day. They offer that enjoyment to their reward center, determining in all good faith that a specific "sigh of relief" moment will be delivered when important time management issues are handled successfully.

Gabe offered himself what appeared to be a very simple thing to look forward to, but he offered this to himself every day. He developed a very detailed picture of himself going to his car at the end of the day and sliding into the driver's seat. He "heard" the door close and the lock engage, and then he sighed with relief, leaning his head against the seat back and momentarily closing his eyes. He was safe at last. Now, Gabe's choice of rewards was very telling, as, the latter part of this imagined scene had him looking in his rearview mirror at the office building he was leaving behind, imagining himself making a rude gesture as he burned rubber leaving the parking lot. However, Gabe's dissatisfaction with his work life was an issue that needed attending to, even as Gabe's readiness to do so increased.

Henry was much more lighthearted in the things he looked forward to. He would contemplate his reunion with his kids at the end of the day, and the thought made him feel relaxed and at peace. He smiled from the inside out as he looked forward to the energy, comfort, and affection he received from each of his six children. Henry, unlike Gabe, thrived in his work place. But like Gabe, Henry struggled to stay on task. Using his own special offering to his reward center helped him to modulate his distractability and to stay productive on task to hasten the moment of going home and being with his family.

How does savoring help with attention deficit? Savoring is attention enhancement. The rule of thumb for making savoring even better: Do it with others; share it; recall it; embellish it. Practicing savoring is building attention related skills and focused thinking. It also broadens the ways in which people practice attending to the details. Savoring quiets the mind and provides for a much needed brain respite for those with hyperactive ADHD brains. Finally, savoring, like narrative and gratitude, helps clients develop a more benign relationship with time. Savoring gives clients the opportunity to differentiate between the past, the present, and the future, finding strength and delight in each temporal mode.

Chapter 8
BEHIND THE CURTAIN

What's in the {Black} Box?

The brain has enjoyed a popular description as the "black box," since no one could safely see inside it, just as no one could see the unconscious. Since the 1990s, called "The Decade of the Brain," amazing advances in brain imaging technology have revealed the structures of the living brain, the activity of the brain at rest and at work Advancements in technology to study cellular molecular structures, and the neurochemicals that affect mood and thought added to progress in unlocking the secrets of the black box. Greater knowledge of genetics and protein channels in the brain added greatly to advancements in neuroscience since the 1990s. As for the unconscious, no imaging technology works to open that aspect of the black box, but self awareness can be increased, often through various types of therapy, the "talking cure."

According to David Cooperrider writing in <u>Appreciative Inquiry: A Positive Revolution in Change </u>(Cooperrider, 2005), it's the question that starts the change. In the case of those with ADHD-like behaviors, a good question to start the change in narrative would be this one: "Why didn't evolution 'select out' the ADHD-type brain?"

Thom Hartmann, with his deep interest in helping people with ADHD, has done some work answering this question. Hartmann has done the service of popularizing and consolidating studies in the area of genetics, evolutionary psychology, anthropology, history, geography, and other fields, compiling this information in his very readable book, <u>The Edison Gene: ADHD and the Gift of the Hunter Child</u> (2003). Hartmann's premise, backed by much research, takes its initial inspiration from the life of prolific inventor Thomas Edison. Young Edison had a crushing experience at the beginning of his formal education. His teacher threw him out of first grade, claiming he was incorrigible, and not bright enough. His mother recognized the harm about to be done to her boy. She began home schooling him from that point on. He was not capable, it is true, to confine his thinking, and his body, to a small desk in a small room. His mother recognized his learning style and created for him opportunities for exploration, movement, and hyperfocus. Edison had a gift. It just looked like a negative condition in certain circumstances, like the classroom.

Positive Psychology pioneer, Mihaly Csikszentmihalyi, former head of The Psychology Department at the University of Chicago, and now at Claremont Graduate University, describes the positive side of hyperfocus as being "flow (1990)." Flow is the experience of timelessness and ultimate engagement. People experiencing flow are experiencing themselves at their best. Flow has elements of just the right amount of challenge, high interest, a sense of competence, and a sense of autonomy.

Hartmann (2003) proposed that the workings of the ADHD brain were selected "in" by evolution because of the usefulness of the type of thinking that helped the human race survive. Supported by many geneticists, the theory is the ADHD behaviors that get students in trouble today may have been an asset to hunters and gatherers of the past.

What is the gene? Thom Hartmann (Hartmann, 2003) called the DRD4 gene the "Edison Gene." Hartmann explains at length that the DRD4 gene is the dopamine receptor D4 gene. This genetic identification, Hartmann admits, is not without some controversy (2003). However, the D4.7 alleles have an established association with ADHD, as indicated in several studies (Manor, 2002), (Langley, 2004).

Hallowell and Ratey note the high occurrence of ADHD in families, at about 75% (2006, pp. 152-155). Most other heritable conditions, they indicate, have about a 50% chance of occurrence. In Delivered from Distraction (2006), Hallowell and Ratey also discuss the recent research in the DRD4 dopamine receptor gene, indicating that about 50% of those diagnosed with ADHD demonstrate abnormalities with dopamine receptors. Dopamine, they point out, is connected to the pleasure center of the brain. Researchers have found that the reward centers of the brain associated with positivity, elevated mood, even with happiness, euphoria, and desire, are activated by dopamine and other neurochemicals called endorphins. Some with ADHD cannot feel adequate pleasure unless they seek high risk, hyper-intense behavior. While inefficient processing of neurotransmitters has an effect on processing speed of information and communication, the dopamine channels are of significance to positive emotions. On the down side, dopamine inefficiently processed, can be as much as 70% higher in those with ADHD than those without (Hallowell & Ratey, Answers to Distraction, 1994). As Hallowell and Ratey point out, this can be an indicator of addictive behaviors of many varieties. At the least, some with ADHD have to engage in exaggerated activities to create enough neurological pleasure just to feel good.

Harvard Medical School's <u>Positive Psychology Health Report</u> (2009) notes the complex process involved with the brain as it is stimulated to feel good. Positive Psychology researchers, like Barbara Fredrickson and Richard Davidson (Fredrickson & Davidson, 2011), have found that the usefulness of the pleasure centers of the brain can be controlled through practices of mindfulness and savoring, among other meditation techniques. This ability to take an active part in modulating dopamine receptors in the brain can enhance and prolong healthy states of happiness. Such ability to change the brain at the prefrontal cortex level, the area for judgment and thinking, can eventually reduce the dangers associated with an imbalance of dopamine and endorphin levels.

Recent developments in neural imagining have made it possible to see the pleasure pathways, according to the <u>Positive Psychology Health Publication</u> (Harvard Health Publications, 2009). Imagining has helped scientists identify the processes of pleasure and happiness, two of the areas of study most frequently associated with Positive Psychology. There is much interest in the field as to how this knowledge can inform the practice of Positive Psychology in areas such as therapy and coaching. Scientists have agreed on the following. Pleasure signals are received in the mid-brain, in a structure identified as the "ventral tegmental area" (VTA). Here's where dopamine comes into play. The VTA controls the release of dopamine into the brain's pleasure center, a structure called the "nucleus accumbens." It is also released into the "amygdala," the brain structure associated with emotions. And very significantly, it also reaches the thinking center of the brain, the area known as the "prefrontal cortex." One more area of the cortex, the "anterior cingulated cortex," is also at work in regulating emotions.

Describing the prefrontal cortex as the brain's seat of critical thinking is credited to Russell Barkley in his work, <u>Attention Deficit Hyperactivity Disorder</u> (1998). He used the now-familiar term "executive function" to describe the overall control this section of the brain exerts overt judgments and other areas of what are called higher order thinking skills. Understanding a good deal about the workings of executive function is important for ADHD coaches. It is a skill set endorsed by the certifying body for coaching, the ICF (International Coach Federation, 2011), as well as by other organizations, like C.H.A.D.D, which support individuals and families with ADHD.

In 2002, Chris A. Zeigler Dendy, wrote a clear synopsis of Barkley's (Barkley, 1998) findings on the role of executive functioning for <u>Attention!</u> Magazine. In it, she compiled a list of the five significant aspects of executive function that, when ineffective, create what has become known as "executive function disorder," which includes many of the thinking differences of people with ADHD (Zeigler Dendy, 2002). However, with help from family, teachers, and practitioners, including therapists and coaches, the five aspects of executive function can operate more harmoniously.

Executive Function Components ((Barkley, 1998) (Zeigler Dendy, 2002)

1. <u>Working Memory and Recall</u>—holding facts in the mind in order to use them in the current situation. Making important connections to stored information. Retrieving information to understand and apply facts.

2. <u>Activation, Arousal and Effort</u>—getting started, paying attention, and finishing.

3. <u>Emotion Control</u>—related to the anterior cingulate cortex—tolerating frustration, controlling impulsive speech and risky actions

4. <u>Internalizing Language</u>—using silent reminders and cues to self-sooth, self-motivate, and direct actions in the future.

5. <u>Complex Problem Solving</u>—analyzing tasks and ideas, breaking them down into manageable "chunks," reorganizing parts to envision the "whole," creating realistic plans to solve problems.

Optimizing the function of these two brain areas , the prefrontal cortex and the anterior cingulated cortex, is particularly significant to clients with ADHD. When the dopamine levels in these areas are under regulated, clients experience the thinking styles and emotional behaviors commonly associated with ADHD. These frequently include forgetfulness, procrastination, and difficulty with prioritizing, distractibility and lack of focus. On the emotional level, some often-noticed negative behaviors include outbursts, contrary behavior, resistance to help, impulsivity, and speaking before thinking.

What are the ADHD-type behaviors that create these difficulties? When frustrated by restrictive environment, behavioral requirements, or non-engaged learning, the results may include boredom, opposition, disruption, impulsivity, risk taking, and sullenness (Hartmann, 2003). On the other hand, circumstances may allow for the "gifts" of the Edison Gene to occur. These may include natural enthusiasm, creativity, curiosity, hyper focus, and leadership, among many other attributes (2003). Non-linear thinking in "hunter-gather" type children and adults often proves to be advantageous to explorers and inventors, like Edison himself.

Like many other researchers studying ADHD and the brain, Dan Amen writes in his recent book, <u>The Amen Solution</u> (2011) that food is medicine. Amen addresses the bad eating habits that develop from an ADHD-type brain that has an overabundance of struggles with impulsiveness, compulsiveness, negativity and sadness, and stress. He lists 50 specific foods that address brain health, from raw almonds to low-fat unsweetened yogurt (2011, p. 329). Amen strongly recommends a diet that includes many plant-based foods that boost concentration and reduce impulsivity. These include richly colored berries, the healthy fat in avocados, and dark green vegetables and green tea. Protein recommendations include quinoa, lean meats, and wild-caught fish high in Omega-3 fatty acids, along with lentils and beans.

What does the latest brain research tell us about diet and the brain? It confirms and adds to the information above. For example, <u>The Neuroscience Quarterly</u> (Society for Neuroscience, 2011) reports on the findings of University of Pennsylvania researcher Teresa Reyes. Her study, "High-Fat Diets Lead to Long-Term Brain Changes" is significant for those with ADHD and with early childhood diets, especially in families with ADHD. This study has implications for the healthy development of reward channels in the brain. Reyes was able to study long term changes in brain structures related to the presence of ADHD. She studied the effects of a high-fat diet in mice. She noticed changes in the nucleus accumbens, ventral tegmental area (VTA), prefrontal cortex, and hypothalamus, considered to be the brain's reward center. Changes occurred in the brain's dopamine transporter, and opioid receptors. Reyes noted how difficult it is to reverse these changes, as they occurred on the molecular level. Even four weeks after the mice were returned to a balance diet, brain changes remained. While it's much easier to support brain health through diet if clients never indulged in high fat content foods, it's certainly advisable that they start. Patience and encouragement are required here, but, though difficult to do, supporting efficient function of the brain's pleasure center is worth the changes in mental clarity that can accompany it.

Those with ADHD should avoid overly processed foods, too much simple sugar, and animal fats and products containing hormones and antibiotics, Dan Amen advises (2011) . The highest quality foods should be consumed. Amen, a long-time practitioner in the field of ADHD diagnosis and treatment, focuses on frontal lobe health, the area that controls decision making and self-regulation. His brain diet recommendations are supported by behavior changes, such as increased positivity, and higher levels of wellbeing and good health. Amen's rule of thumb is the popular concept of eating brightly colored foods, as if picking from the rainbow.

Yet brain studies are not all negative reports for those with ADHD. The question is: How can Positive Psychology coaching, specifically TimeSavor Coaching, acknowledge the negative with compassion, yet help clients bring out the positive?

The Five TimeSavor Brain-Based Recommendations

TimeSavor coaching clients are encouraged to think about their brains with kindness, rather than disappointment. The ADHD brain works very hard all the time. It needs rest and nutrition. Changes in brain health can better occur with as many resources as possible. Habits supporting a deficit model are hard to break. Fortunately, the novelty-seeking brain likes challenges. In this case, the challenge addresses particularly difficult-to-change areas. However, the importance of assisting an over-worked brain is worth the effort. The following recommendations come from the body of cognitive neuroscience research that has increased dramatically since the 1990s "the decade of the brain."

1. Hydrate—The brain is mostly composed of water. Take it out of the desert. The rule of thumb for hydration is to divide your weight by two. The number of the quotient is the number of ounces of water per day clients should try to drink. For example, if you weigh 140, you should try to drink 70 ounces of water during the day. Remembering to do this is a coachable topic!

2. Nourish—Eat the rainbow, creating a colorful and interesting plate, increasing the ratio of plant-based foods to animal products, including dairy.

3. Move—Work you body, build your brain. We are made to walk great distances, so couch-potato-ism isn't compatible with our best selves. ADHD clients are easily addicted to the rapid brain stimulation of computer games and television. Learning to turn it off and move it out is difficult, but part of the entire brain health picture. The ADHD brain benefits from the endorphins released by exercise. It helps to balance out the glucocorticoid stress hormones produced by anxiety and fatigue.

4. Sleep—at least seven hours a day. With the day/night mix up experienced by many ADHD clients, and with the more troublesome over-stimulation of the brain, this is a particularly difficult coaching issue, but one that can produce a great improvement in focus, concentration, and optimism

5. Get Spiritual—Connect to something greater than yourself. Meditate, contemplate, elevate, pray as you will. These give the brain a nice rest in be-

tween tasks. The Rabbi Saul of Tarsus is credited with saying, "Think on all things good and true and beautiful." It was helpful to do this over 2,000 years ago; it's still helpful today.

Remembering to Do Good Things for Yourself

To remember to do good things for your brain and your whole self, the book <u>Mindset</u> (2006) by Stanford psychologist Carol Dweck, offers some guidance. It helps to move the coaching client from a fixed mindset to a growth mindset. Think of opportunities, Dweck advises, plan, and ask the questions: when, where, and how will I make this happen? The growth mindset is more about substantive work for personal improvement, and less concerned with the appearance of doing good work for the approval of others.

To achieve a growth mindset, clients are encouraged to embrace, not fear, challenges. This is a good place for clients to review VIA Signature Strengths scores, considering how to use them with novelty. With the help of exercises in narrative and gratitude, clients enhance strengths of perseverance in the face of obstacles, rather than becoming defensive, blame shifting, or giving up. A common refrain is, "What good is trying? No matter what I do, no one is satisfied." On the other hand, clients' new narratives tell of effort as a means to really reach goals in a timely way.

Criticism is another aspect Dweck writes about (2006). It is certainly a great problem for those whose ADHD behaviors prevent them from using strengths and finding success. Yet, the growth mindset accepts the "even better if…" premise of learning from useful feedback, rather than fearing criticism. Finally, Dweck has observed that, instead of being jealous and threatened by the success of others, the growth mindset can be inspired by the success of others. Clients with ADHD can broaden their thinking about the success of others, to the point of being able to find lessons in others who can actually model desirable strengths.

Distraction Management Strategies

"A.C.T."—This strategy is based on the work of Ellen Langer (Langer, 2011), psychologist and Harvard professor, and colleague of Carol Dweck (Dweck, 2006). To help create mindfulness in the present, and a growth mindset, Langer's research led her to a strategy called "A.C.T." to help develop focus in the face of distractions of all sorts. As adapted, it has been used very effectively by TimeSavor Clients.

- A—"Allow" to interrupt. Only the following should be allowed to turn your mind from your important center of your focused work:
  1. A call from a very important client. Take the call, but set the boundaries. For example, say, "It's so good to hear from you. How can I help right now?" Don't engage in chatting here, but feel free to say, "I'd love to continue this right now, but unfortunately, I'm right in the middle of something. May I call you back later today?" Warning: REMEMBER TO CALL BACK LATER TODAY.
  2. A call from a loved one or close friend. Take the call, but set the boundary, as above. This is not the time to chat, however enticing the prospect may be. Warning: AS ABOVE!

3. An emergency. Attend to that as the priority of the moment. However, check in with your most rational self to make sure of your definition of "emergency." A good way to tell is if it involves, blood, failure to breathe, chest pain, fire or flood, or the like. A sale at the shoe store does not meet the criteria.

- C—"Curtail"—Getting interrupted by chatty co-workers, even chatty bosses merits some positive action. Use the "curtail" tactic as a filter. Clients can ask these questions: Is the conversation in service of my goal? Is this conversation heading someplace I shouldn't go? Then, this is probably not the time to indulge in this activity. As Todd Kashdan (2009) noted, time is finite. Choices on how to allocate this limited resource can and must be made according to the client's availability.

- T—"Triage"—Use a set of standards, or filters, to decide what has to be dealt with immediately, and which items on the "to do" list are less vital for the clients available time. One way is for clients to search out deadlines that are immediately upon them. Another way is to ask: What's fast to do, easy to do, provocative to do, important to do right now (2010). The client can also ask: What can I delegate?

"Triage" can also be filtered using another exercise developed by Michael Bungay Stanier (2010). The client creates three columns on a piece of paper and writes headings:

NEGOTIABLE   NON-NEGOTIABLE   MAYBE   NE-GOTIABLE LATER

What is "negotiable" is what the client choses to put on the day's agenda. The things that are negotiable have a less stringent time constraint than those that are "non-negotible." The agenda items that can only be tackled by the client, which can't be deligated or postponed, and whose deadline is fast approaching, have to find their way to the non-negotiable list. Agenda items that are less vital to that day's agenda may start the day on the "maybe negotiable" list, but may need a review of importance during the day.

Ellen Langer (2011) says there really is no such thing as procrastination. It goes to the concept of "Say Yes To This = Say No To That" (Bungay Stanier, 2010). Langer says it's the choice between one good over another. However, the second place choice does not go away. It still has to be dealt with sooner rather than later. It will come back on the "to do" list until it gets the "Say Yes To This" treatment.

Some scientists, and clients, still refer to lack of timely productivity. Here are the thoughts of another Harvard researcher on the subject. An expert on procrastination and mindfulness is Sharon Melnick. Melnick is a psychologist and coach who has come up with a list of seven types of procrastinators. Reviewing this list helps clients to become more aware of habits of a fixed mindset. With this starting point, clients can apply strengths based exercises and tools to develop a growth, or "productivity," mindset with which to better arrive at their goals.

Seven Types of Procrastinators (Melnick, 2011)

1. **Perfectionists**—stop working before they even start, because their mindset insists that they will never produce a perfect product. The productivity mindset: Not perfect, but done. It's better to be done than be perfect. Perfect is never done. Mel-

nick suggests that Perfectionists try using the 80-20 rule. They should make decisions, rather than putting them off. They can trust that their judgment will be correct 80% of the time, and that the other 20% can be "even better if..." learning experiences. Melnick suggests another useful strategy for perfectionists to go along with the "Not perfect but done" growth mindset. It's called "Draft + Eyes On + Revision." It helps Perfectionists to think of their work as a draft. The key element that changes productivity is for clients to choose someone they trust to put "eyes on" the work in progress. When that person "volleys back" the work to the client, the client commits to quickly produce the revisions and volley them right back to their "eyes on" the reader. The reader becomes another voice saying, "Not perfect, but done."

2. **Avoiders**—There is something "too much" about the task that has clients' mindsets fixed on making excuses and delaying the choice to get busy. For example, a task is too difficult for just one person, but no one is willing to help; a task will take too long; a task will use up too much energy; a task has too many complications; a task is too boring. The productivity mindset: clients should challenge the assumptions. What if a task is NOT "too" anything, but actually an opportunity similar to other successes clients have experienced? What are some of the clients' strengths that could be brought to bear? What if tackling this challenge will bring a rewarding sigh of relief. What if completing this task will bring about something the client can look forward to? And, is it really true that no one will help?

3. **Dreamers**—As the heading indicates, dreamers are really good at one of the 4 Ds of Appreciative Inquiry (Cooperrider, 2005), that is, the dreaming stage. They are underdeveloped in the destiny stage, the part of a project that reaches the goal. Dreamers make the mistake of thinking that mental plotting of amazing and varied connections and opportunities are the equivalent of actually doing those things. They rarely try to count the cost of their dreams, or consider unintended consequences. They ARE valuable team members, and their insights and visions are compelling. But their inattention to details and realistic constraints is disappointing and annoying to others. The productivity mindset: Seek the help of a detail-oriented person. Clients should continue to dream, but they must commit to the destiny phase as well. Their self-question: How does this dream become a fulfilled destiny? What are my first steps? What steps come next, and who will do them, by when? (Whitworth, Kimsey-House, & Sandhal, 1998).

4. **Protectors**—Clients with the style of procrastination haven't developed an adequate sense of confidence. They don't stretch or reach for fear of criticism. They would prefer to protect the *status quo,* and truly make excuses for not putting themselves or their work out there. Productivity mindset: Build confidence by increasing awareness of strengths. Narrate the stories of success. Recall what was learned from short-comings and design ways to avoid the same pit falls. Renew the mind regarding criticism. It doesn't have the power to wound the client. The work product is not the same thing as the client. The productivity mind-

set can see the "even better if…" side to criticism. It can be an opportunity to learn.

5. **Pressure lovers**—These clients have the mindset that they can never do anything until the last minute. They need that endorphin rush more than they need the sigh of relief or the Ah-ha's that come with a timely finish. Now, if their work product squeeks in under the wire, and if their work product is excellent, then perhaps there is nothing to complain about. But how often is this the case? Pressure lovers can learn to modulate their need for neurochemical highs. Mindfulness, savoring, and meditation can help develop a growth mindset that can find pleasure rewards in a more helpful way. Creating a high level of stress is ultimately physically unhealthy. It is certainly distructive to relationships as well.

6. **Prioritizers**—Clients like this make lists. And these lists contain all the possible items that have to be done <u>first</u> before the actual goal of the project ever gets on the "to do" agenda. Prioritizers really are very insightful. They are like hunters stalking elusive prey, picking up the tiniest details, unseen by many others. The downside to this is their mindset becomes rigidly fixed on "but first" list items to the exclusion of any productive movement toward next steps. Often, they combine this with the Avoiders style, indicating that the items that have to be done first are just "too…" difficult, dependent on unavailable help, complicated, and so forth. One other problem with these "but first" lists is that Prioirtzers are the sole determiners of what is important. They don't seek input from others as to what <u>they</u> might actually consider im-

portant, differing in spirit and substance from the Prioritizers' fixed list. The productivity mindset in this case first challenges all the "but first" assumptions, asking, Is it really true that we have to do all this first? Is there a more stream-lined path to action? The second step is to seek out the needs of others involved. Challenge the clients' assumptions that they have cornered the market on what's best for everyone. They might learn to trust and appreciate the "even better if..." potential that comes from more than one brain approaching a mutual goal.

7.   **ADHD**—Melnick includes this title for the seventh type of procrastination because of its unique neurological aspects. The prefrontal cortex delays in development affect good long term thinking and planning. The dopamine channels and endorphins make it more than difficult to "Say Yes" to hard challenges and "Say No" to pleasures. Fear of criticsm is very justified among ADHD clients, and it tends to make them Protectors. Why step out if all that awaits are *ad hominem* attacks? Melnick sees procrastination based on ADHD neurological determinates as quickly shifting from one to another of her previously listed six categories. What changes the ADHD mindset is to utilize the suggestions for developing a productivity mindset as each style of procrastination emerges. Awareness of the procrastinating behavior as laid out in Melnick's list is a very good conversation starter between coach and client. Narratives of times of success, using strengths in new ways, learning to savor time for the pleasurable experiences savoring can bring, and practicing gratitude as a way

of building more respectful bonds with others, are all coaching strategies that can help ADHD clients.

As David Cooperrider notes in <u>Appreciative Inquiry</u> (2005), it is the question that starts the change. In this case, the inquiry starts with: "Why didn't evolution 'select out' the ADHD-type brain?" This type of inquiry has self-appreciation in mind. Self-appreciation is quite a novel approach for those with a self-condemning mindset related to ADHD behaviors. ADHD sufferers who have historically repeated the story of what goes wrong become alienated. What becomes clear is that the gifts and strengths of these people are suppressed as well. Recall here the story of Edison in his elementary school classroom. On the other hand, the story of what goes right can commence with the idea that ADHD thinking is not exclusively a deficit, but has value and purpose in many endeavors and circumstances.

Chapter 9
COMMENCEMENT

...And sorrow and mourning shall fade away

Struggles with ADHD behaviors, around timeliness in particular, bear a similarity to sorrow and loss. When looked at through a deficit model, ADHD is a neurological disorder, often accompanied by depression and anxiety. De-normalization of the PERSON, not just the behaviors of that person, adds to a profound sense of loss for parents. Their heart-felt dreams for their children disappear into the worlds of social stigma and academic struggles. They grieve for what isn't, as do so many parents who experience loss. Within this mental mindset, children grow to believe they have lost the "normal" life. They can't articulate it, but they absorb the loss of the child their family never had, the child they aren't. Deficit-model perception does all this and more. Without positive and effective intervention, their life path is marked by sadness and alienation. The bonds of connectedness are generally underdeveloped. They long for what they don't have: a full cup of autonomy, competence, and good relationships.

Sari Solden, psychotherapist specializing in the treatment of adults with ADHD and their partners, has written in <u>Women With Attention Deficit Disorder</u> (1995), that after the diagnosis of ADHD, clients feel relief. It feels good to know what goes on with their thinking actually has a name. However, Solden notes quite accurately that the Grief Cycle fairly quickly follows the feeling of relief. Solden explains that the Grief Cycle, denial, anger, bargaining, depression, and acceptance, applies to ADHD clients in very specific ways (pp. 170-172).

After the diagnosis, clients may deny that there really is such a thing as ADHD. They may question whether or not they really have it. It takes a while for people to become comfortable with this change in self-concept, and to integrate a more positive view of a different way of thinking into their lives.

After denial, anger emerges from the realization that they have had ADHD for a long time, but the best practices for help and support were not there for them. How infuriating that many professionals had ideas about how to help them, but they have gone for years, into their adulthood without knowing such support existed.

Adults with ADHD bargain that as long as they take medication, they will be fine. But best treatment practices come with the inclusion of behavior management, therapy, and coaching. It takes more than a pill to create a more fulfilling and happier life, Solden (1995) explains.

Clients can show signs of disappointment with the results of medication, or setbacks in goal achievement lead clients to feelings of depression. They feel they have lost so much time addressing their symptoms. They have lost opportunities for better relationships with others because they didn't have a toolbox of strategies for curbing impulsiveness, moderating communication, and keeping to schedules and appointments. It is not easy to make these necessary changes, but adult clients often go through a period of isolation and loneliness. Grief is expressed as feelings of loss over all the missed opportunities, hopes, and dreams.

TimeSavor clients have experienced this grief cycle as well. It is very important for them to understand the progression toward changes and meeting goals comes with a sense of loss. Tears are shed; fury is expressed. Clients back away from their diagnosis, then move in closer with a reframing that ADHD is not always a deficit. They try to bargain it away, offering tokens of compliance, but returning now and then to ineffective models of thinking, choosing familiarity over change at times. TimeSavor clients do experience periods of depression. They often work with a therapist along with their coach. The best outcome is that more and more frequently, as these clients revisit stages of the grief cycle, they experience acceptance of their different brain. They learn the benefit of caring for their brain with loving kindness, accepting that it's style and structures are part of human evolution for good reason.

However, when the deficit and disease model is challenged, what can change for these families and individuals? Researchers and practitioners, working within the ADHD community, are beginning to understand the ADHD brain in a strengths based model, that is, as a gift rather than a deficit. Likewise, Positive Psychology researchers and practitioners understand more each day about a growth model for life changing wellbeing and flourishing. The courageous questioning of the *status quo* has allowed for this question: "What goes right with people...with ADHD?" The resulting science and research has found a welcoming home within the discipline of coaching. Coaching is one of the first professions in which Positive Psychology has been applied.

Positive Psychology, as a distinct discipline and area of practice, is beginning its second decade. ADHD coaching has recently developed standards for advanced certification. When these two disciplines align, a distinct coaching model, TimeSavor Coaching, emerges. What begins, then, is in service of life satisfaction, especially as it relates to those time-specific difficulties commonly recognized within the constellation of ADHD behaviors. What begins is a mindset change from negativity, critical self-talk, sorrow, shame and loss, to a strengths-based positive outlook.

Positive Psychology research has multiple trajectories. These include multidisciplinary studies and applications into what makes life worth living, what works well in people, and the importance of other people in creating a truly happy life. Areas of current Positive Psychology practice include Positive Education, Positive Work Place, Positive Families, Positive Communities, and Positive Cross- Cultural Understanding.

The way practitioners and clients think about ADHD is beginning to change as well. The new look of ADHD is coming from a strengths-based model, a version of Positive Psychology's "what goes right with people?" thematic approach to wellbeing, flourishing and happiness. Controlling ADHD behaviors is difficult for all involved. Trying to support ADHD brain differences, on the other hand, offers new opportunities for working with thinking styles rather than against them. The emerging model for ADHD help is moving from a deficit model to a strengths based one. While ADHD is still a diagnosed neurological condition, more people are entertaining the idea that the ADHD brain has qualities that are useful for human survival. These characteristics are deficits in specific circumstances, such as classrooms, office cubbies, and other more structured, restrictive environments. In other circumstances, those that support kinesthetic learning, curiosity, and novel thinking, the ADHD brain is at an advantage.

There are circumstances, however, in which clients with ADHD are not readily at their best. Even so, they still desire to be on time, to create reachable goals, keep appointments, and finish projects. They still wish to accommodate the schedule of others, and feel diminished and criticized when they don't measure up in these areas.

Offering a new kind of support for time related issues, Positive Psychology coaching changes the language from "fix" to "flow." What if a new way was to tell about strength-based relationships with the entire concept of time, a kind of "temporal confluence"? What if appreciations for the past, present, and even future, replaced anger, fear, and ingratitude? What if time is not something to be "managed," but rather savored? What if coaching applied PERMA, and used SDT research?

And, what might a "Once Upon a Time..." narrative sound like, if it were compiled from the stories of the TimeSavor coaching clients we've met within these pages? The following story, compiled from stories of many TimeSavor clients, might sound like this:

"Once Upon A Time...And Then...Finally": A Composite Story

Once upon a time, there were ten different people who had something in common. They were all diagnosed with ADHD when they were adults.

Their names weren't really Jack, Nikki, Nathan, Lucy, Tom, Janice, Gabe, Allen, Henry, and Larry, but that's how they've been known so far. For ease of identification in this story, they will be known as "The Ten." The Ten, whose composite story this is, had something else in common. They didn't like themselves, and other people didn't like them that much either. The reason for this dislike was that The Ten really didn't do very well when it came to self-regulation around issues related to time. They were sad, called themselves failures, didn't fit in with others, and didn't believe they could change the way their minds worked. Their brains were broken. Doctors told them they had a neurological disorder.

Another thing The Ten had in common was that they would often impulsively take on commitments they had no time to keep. They would also make promises to people, and then forget about those promises almost immediately. They'd forget about the people, too. Then, they'd try to avoid the broken-promise people, along with customers, creditors, relatives, and friends who wanted to reach them. When The Ten tried to focus on important tasks, especially ones they didn't like doing, their skin would crawl, they'd feel claustrophobic, and they'd seek distraction. Often, though, distraction sought them. After all, what could they do? Their brains were broken.

And then, someone got really tired of enduring The Ten's undesirable behaviors. So, this person [boss, wife, husband, mother, professor, relative or friend] issued the ultimatum: "Get help or get lost. You've tried psychiatrists, therapists, medication, and diets. The only thing left for you to try is coaching, so get an ADHD coach. Now. Today." They liked the idea of working with a Positive Psychology coach who knew the special needs of people with ADHD.

Positive Psychology focused on strengths. They took strengths assessments and were surprised that they had something good to contribute. The Ten hadn't thought in these terms. During this process, they learned more about ADHD, and were intrigued by the idea that ADHD thinking could be creative, resourceful, artistic, imaginative, and inventive, along with many other attributes. Not everyone views the ADHD brain as a disordered brain. Some scientists see it as a brain that played an important part in the survival of the race.

The Ten were coached using appreciative narrative, along with exercises in gratitude, and savoring. Slowly, in very small steps, The Ten changed focus from "what goes wrong" to what can be "even better if." From the outset, the Positive Psychology coaching question for them was, "What are you good at?" This turned out to be a unique coaching approach, specifically designed with the needs of ADHD clients in mind.

Finally, all of them began to hush the sound of their inner critics. They replaced them with the "voices" of their heroes of the heart. Ruminating over past failures gave way to stories of times they were at their best, and to stories about a brighter future. They practiced ways to savor time, not hate it, and they became less resistant to change. They learned that practicing gratitude helped them develop good relationships with people. It opened their hearts and lifted their minds. Then, they learned over time how to strengthen the concept that other people mattered. Because that was so, they showed up on time and kept promises more and more often. The Ten practiced sorting out commitments, then sticking to the ones closest to their goals and values. The Ten liked their brains more, and treated their brains with more loving kindness.

Not everybody gets to live happily ever after, but at least The TimeSavor Ten would be very pleased to say they could live more happily more of the time. Knowing that a cup of tea tastes good is a fine place to start.

WORKS CITED

Amen, D. (1998). Change Your Brain, Change Your Life. NY: Three Rivers Press.

Amen, D. (2011). The Amen Solution: the Secret to Being Thinner, Smarter, Happier. NY: Crown Archetype.

Barkley, R. (1998). Attention Deficit Hyperactivity disorder. NY: The Guildford Press.

Ben-Shahar, T. (2007). Happier: Learn the Secrets to Daily Joy and Lasting Fulfillment. NY: McGraw-Hill.

Biswas-Diener, R. (2008). An Invitation to Positive Psychology: Research and Tools for the Professional. London, UK: British Library Cataloguing-in-Publication Data.

Biswas-Diener, R. (2010). Practicing Positive Psychology Coaching: Assessments, Activities, and Strategies for Success. Hoboken, NJ: John wiley & Sons.

Biswas-Diener, R. (2009). Work Style Scale.

Biswas-Diener, R., & Dean, B. (2007). Positive Psychology Coaching: Putting the Science of Happiness to Work for Your Clients. Hoboken, NY: John Wiley & Sons.

Bryant, F. (2009). Savoring Beliefs Inventory (SBI): A scale for measuring beliefs about savoring. Journal of Mental Health, 12, 175-196.

Bryant, F., & Veroff, J. (2007). Savoring: A New Model of Positive Experience. Mahwah, NJ, US: Lawrence Erlbaum Associates.

Bryant, F., & Yeroff, J. (2007). Savoring: A New Model of Positive Experience. Mahwah, NJ: Lawrence Erlbaum Associates.

Bungay Stanier, M. (2010). Do More Great WorkNY. Workman Publishing.

Cooperrider, D. L. (2005). Appreciative Inquiry: A Positive Revolution in change. San Francisco, CA, USA: Berret-Koehler.

Csikszentmihalyi, M. (1990). Flow: The Psychology of Optimal Experience. NY: Harper Perennial.

Dean, B. MentorCoach. Retrieved July 12, 2011, from MentorCoach Coach Training Web site: http://www.mentor-coach.com

Deci, E. L., & Ryan, R. (2002). The Handbook of Self Determination Research. Rochester, NY: University of Rochester Press.

Dweck, C. (2006). Mindset: the New Psychology of Success. NY: Ballantine Books.

Emmons, R. (2007). Thanks! How The New Science of Gratitude Can Make You Happier. NY: Houghton Mifflin.

Fredrickson, B. (2009). Positivity. NY: Crown Publishing.

Fredrickson, B., & Davidson, R. (2011). Pathbreaking Findings from the Science of Meditation. SecondWorld Congress on Positive Psychology. July 23-26. Philadelphia: International Positive Psychology Association.

Govindji, R., & Linley, A. (2007). Strengths use, self-concordance, and wellbeing: Implications for strengths coaching and coaching psychologists. International Coaching Psychology Review 2, 143-153.

Grant Halvorson, H. (2010). Succeed: How We Can Reach Our Goals. NY: Hudson Street Press.

Hallowell, E., & Ratey, J. (1994). Answers to Distraction. NY: Pantheon Books.

Hallowell, E., & Ratey, J. (2006). Delivered from Distraction: Getting the Most out of Life with Attention Deficit Disorder. NY: Ballantine Books.

Hartmann, T. A. (2003). The Edison Gene: ADHD and the Gift of the Hunter Child. Rochester, Vermont, USA: Park Street Press.

Harvard Health Publications. (2009). Positive Psychology Special Health Report. Harvard Medical School. Boston: Harvard Health Publications.

Hirari, T. O. (2011). Sorry, I Can't Find Anything Positive in Me!!: How to Effectively Conduct Positive Psychology Interventions for Negatively-Minded People. Second WprldCongress on Positive Psychology. July 23-26. Philadelphia: International Positive Psychology Association.

International Coach Federation. (2011). ICF Core Competencies. Retrieved August 1, 2011, from ICF the International Coach Federation: http://www.coachfederation.org

International Positive Psychology Association (IPPA). (2009). Welcome to IPPA Network On Line. Retrieved July 09, 2011, from IPPA Network Web site: http://www. ippanetwork.org

Joseph, S., & Linley, A. (2007). Trauma, Recovery, and Growth: Positive Psychological Perspectives on Posttraumatic Stress. Hoboken, NJ: John Wiley & Sons.

Kashdan, T. (2009). Curious? Discover the Missing Ingredient to a Fulfilling Life. NY: William Morrow.

Kelm, J. (2005). Appreciative Living: The Principles of Appreciative Inquiry. Wake Forest, NC: Venet Publishers.

King, L. (2001, July). The health benefits of writing about life goals. Personality and Social Psychology Bulletin, 27 (7), pp. 798-807.

114

Langer, E. (2011). Ellen Langer Blog. (B. Dean, Producer, & MentorCoach) Retrieved from Ellen Langer: htcp://www.ellen-langer.com/blog/152/ben-dean-interview

Langley, K. v. (2004). Association of the dopamine D4 receptor gene 7-epeat allele with neuropsychological test performance of children with ADHD. American Journal of Psychiatry, 1, 133-8.

Lyubomirsky, S. (2007). The How of Happiness: A Scientific Approach to Getting the Life You Want. NY: Penguin Books.

Manor, I. T.-M. (2002). The short DRD4 repeats confer risks to attention deficit hyperactivity disorder in a family-based design and impair performance on a continuous performance test. Molecular Psychiatry , 7 (7), 790-4.

McCarney, S. B. (1994). The Attention Deficit Disorders Intrvention Manual, 2nd Edition. Columbia, MO: Hawthorne Educational Services.

Melnick, S. (2011). Productivity Mindset Mastery. Retrieved from Productivity Mndset Mastery: http://www.productivitymindsetmastery.com

Niemiec, R. (2011). After the VIA Survey: Next Steps for Coaches and Clinicians. 2nd Internatiional Positive Psychology Association Congress, July 25. Philadelphia.

Orem, S. B. (2007). Appreciative Coaching: A Positive Process for Change. San Francisco: Jossey-Bass.

Peterson, C. (2006). A Primer in Positive Psychology. NY: Oxford University Press.

Peterson, C., & Seligman, M. (2004). Character Strengths and Virtues: A Handbook and Classification. NY, USA: American Psychological Association and Oxford University Press.

Prochaska, J., Norcross, J., & DiClemente, C. (2002). Changing For Good: A Revolutionary Six-Stage Program for Overcoming Bad Habits ad Moving Your Life Positively Forward. NY: Avon.

Rock, D., & Page, L. (2009). Coaching with The Brain in Mind: Foundations for Practice. Hoboken, NJ: John Wiley & Sons.

Sapolsky, R. (1998). Why Zebras Don't Get Ulcers. NY: W.H. Freeman.

Seligman, M. (2002). Authentic Happiness: Using the New Positive Psychology to Realize Your Potential for Lasting Fulfillment. NY, USA: Free Press.

Seligman, M. (2011). Flourish: A Visionary New Understanding of Happiness and Well-Being. NY: Free Press.

Siegel, R.E. (2009). Positive Psychology Health Report: Harnessing the Power of Happiness, Personal Strength, and Mindfulness. Harvard Health Publications, Harvard Medical School. Boston: Harvard Medical School.

Society for Neuroscience. (2011). Neuroscience Quarterly. Washington, D.C.: Society for Neuroscience.

Solden, S. (1995). Women with Attention Deficit Disorder. Grass Valley, CA: Underwood Books.

Teeter Ellison, P. (2003, June). AD/HD Myths: Science Over Criticism. ATTENTION!

Whitworth, L., Kimsey-House, H., & Sandhal, P. (1998). Co-Active Coaching: New Skills for Coaching People Toward Success in Work and Life. Mounain View, CA: Davies-Black Publishing.

Wood, A., Linley, A., Maltby, J., Baliousis, M., & Joseph, S. (2008). The authentic personality: A theoretical and empirical conceptualization and the development of the authenticity scale. Journal of Counseling Psychology , 55, 385-399.

Wrzesniewski, M. C., Rozin, P., & Schwartz, B. (1997). Jobs, careers, ad calings: Peoples' relations to their work. Journal of Research in Personality , 31, 22-33.

Young, J., & Giwerc, D. (2003, December). Just What Is Coaching? Attention!

Zeigler Dendy, C. (2002, February). Five Components of Executive Function and How They Impact Shool Performance. Attention!

Dr. Virginia M. Hurley

Virginia began her career in education as an English teacher in the New York City public schools. Her work led her to become a teacher trainer, and later, an administrator. Upon retiring from a career in public education, Virginia completed training as a life coach. She became a certified life coach, using her experiences as teacher, teacher trainer, and administrator in her coaching practice.

She specializes in Positive Psychology Coaching, primarily in the areas of time management, goal setting, and transitions.

She lives with her family in the Lower Hudson Valley area of New York State.

Made in the USA
Charleston, SC
10 March 2012